ICNC Press

EDITORS: Hardy Merriman and Amber French
Contact: icnc@nonviolent-conflict.org
DESIGNER: Joe García

Published by ICNC Press
International Center on Nonviolent Conflict
600 New Hampshire Ave. NW, Ste. 710
Washington, D.C. 20037 USA

© 2018, 2021
International Center on Nonviolent Conflict,
Ivan Marovic
All rights reserved.

First edition: 2018
Second edition: 2021
ISBN (Paperback): 978-1-943271-37-5

Cover Photo: Ivan Marovic serving as a battering ram to break the door of the Deanery at the Belgrade University during the 1996-1997 Student Protest. Photo by Miroslav Petrovic.

Copyright Page Photo: Euromaidan demonstrations in Kiev, Ukraine on December 29, 2013. Photo by Maksymenko Oleksander. Licensed under CC BY 2.0. The image has been modified by cropping. https://creativecommons.org/licenses/by/2.0/

Publication Disclaimer: The designations used and material presented in this publication do not indicate the expression of any opinion whatsoever on the part of ICNC. The author holds responsibility for the selection and presentation of facts contained in this work, as well as for any and all opinions expressed therein, which are not necessarily those of ICNC and do not commit the organization in any way.

THE PATH OF MOST **RESISTANCE**

A STEP-BY-STEP GUIDE TO PLANNING NONVIOLENT CAMPAIGNS

Second Edition

Table of Contents

Foreword by Hardy Merriman 1

Introduction 3

1. Nonviolent Civil Resistance Campaigns 5

2. SWOT Analysis: Understanding Your Current Capabilities and the Environment 13

3. Scenario Development: Anticipating Possible Outcomes 23

4. SMART Criteria: Setting Campaign Objectives 35

5. Spectrum of Allies: Mapping Stakeholders 45

6. Perception Box: Analyzing Stakeholders' Beliefs and Feelings 55

7. Brainstorming: Conjuring Up Tactics 67

8. Cost/Benefit Analysis: Picking the Best Idea 75

9. Campaign Plan: Putting it All on Paper 85

10. Tactics 95

11. Campaign Development Course 109

12. Tactical Planning Workshop 117

Afterword 121

Tables and Figures

Table 1: SWOT Matrix 16

Table 2: Examples of Strengths, Weaknesses, Opportunities, and Threats 18

Table 3: Scenario Development 26

Table 4: Examples of BC, MO, CT, and WC Scenarios 28

Figure 1: Strategy, Campaigns, and Tactics 7

Figures 2 & 3: Blueprints .... 8 & 9

Figure 4: Plan A and Plan B 29

Figure 5: Spectrum of Allies 48

Foreword
by Hardy Merriman

I remember hearing the name of Serbian autocrat Slobodan Milosevic in the 1990s. It was spoken regularly on the news in the United States. Sometimes referred to as "The Butcher of the Balkans," Milosevic persecuted his political opponents and later went on trial for genocide, war crimes, and crimes against humanity. When his military engaged in ethnic cleansing in Kosovo in 1999, NATO led a bombing campaign against Yugoslavia. The bombs got Milosevic to withdraw his forces, but they did not get him out of power.

Yet his dictatorship toppled in October 2000. The society he had ruled for more than a decade launched a popular nonviolent movement for democracy that proved more powerful than his regime. A group called *Otpor* ("Resistance"), which was started by Serbian youth and expanded rapidly, played a critical role in this process.

Otpor was developed by a dozen young activists, and it grew over the course of two years to include tens of thousands of people from across Serbia. Spreading in a decentralized way and localizing in communities across the country, Otpor moved people from political apathy to political mobilization. It emphasized training new recruits, transmitting a culture of activism, and developing innovative nonviolent actions (including a wide range of protests, and later, strikes and boycotts) to make Milosevic's dictatorship unsustainable. Otpor was bold, smart, and resourceful—and it succeeded.

Ivan Marovic was one of the original Otpor leaders, and he has the stories, wisdom, and lived experience of those critical years waging nonviolent civil resistance against dictatorship. He also has insights and lessons from being a leading trainer and thinker in the field of civil resistance for the last two decades, engaging with movements fighting oppression in countries around the world.

I highly recommend this powerful book. Ivan's presentation is logical and structured. He offers no formula for success (each activist has unique circumstances that they must navigate for themselves), but he shares key questions and exercises to help readers develop their own answers about how to organize effective nonviolent campaigns. If you are willing to put in the work, this book will help you and your fellow activists in your own journey, and sharpen your strategy in the fight for rights, freedom, and justice.

Introduction

If you asked me about the movement I was part of, Otpor, and the campaigns we ran, I could tell you a lot about the "Gotov Je" (He's Finished) and "Vreme Je" (It's Time) campaigns, aimed at increasing voter turnout at the September 24, 2000 presidential election in Serbia. The election was a prelude to the ultimate downfall of Slobodan Milosevic on October 5 the same year. I could tell you about the "We're Watching You" campaign we ran right after the downfall of Milosevic, the purpose of which was to position Otpor as a watchdog closely monitoring the performance of the new government and distancing ourselves from it. I could tell you about the "Fist is the Salute" campaign, with the objective to increase Otpor recruitment and which ended with thousands joining the movement.

I could talk about all of these at length, but I couldn't name a single campaign that we ran in the first year of our existence. I could talk about tactics all day long ("actions" as we called them). I could also talk about the Declaration on the Future of Serbia, Otpor's strategic document. But I couldn't name a single campaign from our first year.

Why? Because there were none.

Otpor was tactically very innovative from the start and developed a long-term strategy within months of its foundation, but it took us some time to learn how to run campaigns.

This is because campaigns are difficult to plan and implement. In my view, campaign planning requires more effort than long-term strategic planning and short-term tactical planning for several reasons. First, a strategic plan is usually broad enough to accommodate changing environments and unexpected turns of events that may occur during strategy roll-out (usually measured in years). On the other hand, tactical planning is short enough (usually measured in days or sometimes weeks) for results to be observed and evaluated, necessary modifications to be made, and new, innovative, and improved tactics to be introduced.

But campaigns are different. Unlike strategy, they need to be detailed, their objectives specific, their targets well defined, and their messages clear and straightforward. Campaigns must correspond to changing environments but must also support the long-term strategy. And since it takes time for campaigns to have an effect, it is more difficult to evaluate them. Unlike tactics, you must wait months before making changes based on an evaluation of the campaign's effectiveness.

When poor planning produces ineffective campaigns, you face a tough choice—to continue an ineffective campaign or to abort it. It is my hope that this guide will help you avoid this undesirable position.

This planning guide covers a number of tools that help you answer the most important campaign questions:

1. What do you want to achieve (what is the campaign objective)?

2. What are you going to say (what is the campaign message)?

3. What are you going to do (which tactics are you going to carry out)?

4. What do you need in terms of resources and organization?

Tools in this guide aim to help activists and organizers better understand their internal capabilities and external environment, formulate appropriate objectives, define target audiences and analyze their perceptions, formulate a message, and decide which tactics are optimal for conveying this message.

Each tool is introduced and explained in greater detail for those who have never used it before. This explanation is followed by a step-by-step account of how to use the tool in a workshop, whether it is a training workshop aimed at teaching participants about campaigns or a planning workshop with the aim of devising a specific campaign. In this sense, it is suitable for experienced and inexperienced activists alike, and is designed to be useful at all stages of a nonviolent movement for rights, justice, and freedom.

Tools are accompanied by modules that all together will take approximately 12 hours to complete—for example, during a weekend-long campaign planning workshop. All materials needed to conduct such a workshop are identified in the respective modules and are available (or acceptable alternatives) at minimal material cost in most areas of the world.

1. NONVIOLENT CIVIL RESISTANCE CAMPAIGNS

What are Campaigns, and Why Are They Important?

The root of the word is from the Latin "campus" or field. Armies used to go out in the field in the spring to conduct campaigns—major operations that were part of a larger war effort. This term is still used by soldiers today. Even outside the military—in business, marketing, politics, and so forth—campaigns refer to a series of activities intended to achieve a particular objective within a larger strategy. Strategy therefore consists of different operations, including campaigns, which themselves consist of a number of tactics, also commonly referred to as actions or tasks. Tactics make up campaigns, and campaigns—along with other operations such as recruitment, training, internal and external communications—are used in service of strategy (see Figure 1).

Figure 1: Strategy, Campaigns, and Tactics

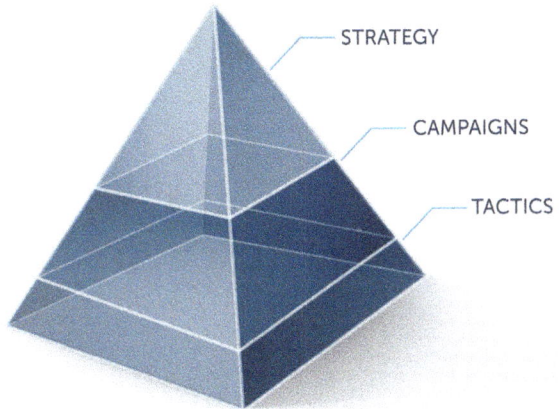

> *Civil resistance is a way for ordinary people who have no special title, status, or privilege to wield power without the use or threat of physical violence.*

Campaigns serve to mobilize and engage specific audiences. They aim to change the views, perceptions, and even behaviors of the general public. Campaigns are therefore critical if your strategy depends on increasing public participation, which is usually the case with political strategy.

This is true for institutional politics (like lobbying) and is especially true if the struggle is waged outside of institutions, as is the case with civil resistance by definition.

It is often remarked that activists prioritize tactics over strategy. Even when a strategy has been developed, there is often a disconnect between strategic and tactical levels, or activists may plan one thing in the strategy room but improvise in the streets. Activists who have produced a strategy often still wonder which specific steps will take them toward that strategy. They may continue using familiar tactics while the strategic plan is never fully implemented.

Campaigns are useful because they can serve as a link between strategy and tactics. After completing your strategic plan, you don't need to get into tactical detail just yet. You can first define campaigns as broader phases of the strategy. Objectives of each campaign will serve as milestones on the road to the strategic goal and you will be able to divide this road into shorter segments.

How Are Strategy, Campaigns, and Tactics Related? Why Are They Interdependent?

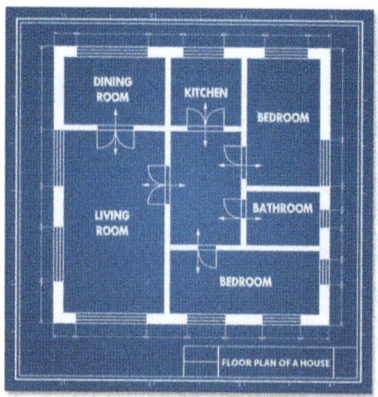

Figure 2

Think of strategy as a house, then campaigns as different rooms in that house. Tactics can be understood as construction elements—walls, windows, doors, and furniture. These elements can exist outside the house but they are not very useful on their own. When you use these elements inside the house, they are used differently in each room, depending on the function of the room. For example, usually there is a door between a kitchen and a dining room, but there may not be a door between a kitchen and a bedroom (see Figure 2).

The same can be said about tactics. You can organize a tactic without a strategy, but it is not very useful. Even within a wider strategy, tactics should be part of a particular campaign, executed to convey that campaign's message and to impact a specific target audience.

Unlike tactics, campaigns cannot exist without strategy—like rooms cannot exist without the house. Even a one-room house is still a house; it has foundations and a roof. In the same manner, strategy with one campaign is still a strategy; it has a defined vision, mission, and goals. An optimal house is of course sturdy, but also functional. For the latter to be true, an optimal room layout is necessary. Strategy needs vision, mission, and goals, but it also needs campaigns to be functional.

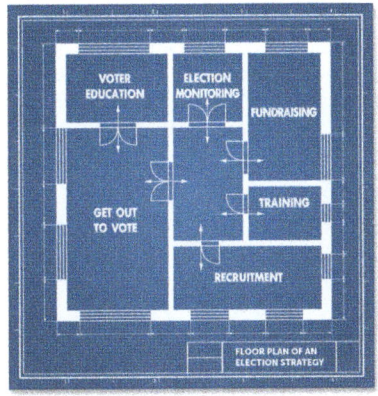

Figure 3

Each room in the house serves a particular purpose, but they are interconnected in terms of function and construction. The kitchen and the dining room are adjacent because of their function—prepared food should not travel long before it is served. The design of the house is intentional and serves specific, connected purposes.

The same is true for campaigns. In a broader strategy, campaigns follow each other as steps toward the long-term goal. They also build on each other, as later campaigns use the gains that previous campaigns achieve (see Figure 3).

If we take election strategy as an example, a Get Out to Vote campaign occupies the central place of the "floor plan" but is supported by other operations such as election monitoring and voter education. "The roof" is the vision of free and fair elections and the "foundation" is the mission of promoting active participation of citizens in the election process. "Furniture" in this "house" consists of tactics such as town-hall meetings, workshops for election observers, door-to-door canvassing, and so forth.

Longer, more complex strategies have more elaborate "floor plans" with many "rooms," "corridors," and "stairways." Simple strategies have one or two "rooms," but they are all characterized by the same interdependence between strategy, campaigns, and tactics.

The goal of this guide is to help you develop a campaign plan in support of your broader strategy (which is a topic that will be covered later in a separate book). This campaign plan will be the result of a process involving careful analysis and creative thinking. Tools in this guide will help you with both and lead you step-by-step toward a campaign plan. And once you complete your campaign plan, you will be able to derive other useful documents, such as a campaign brief, calendar, budget, and organizational chart.

Case Study: Otpor's "He's Finished" and "It's Time" Campaigns

The "Gotov Je" (He's Finished) campaign was Otpor's primary (but not only) voter mobilization campaign. Its broad objective was to bring down Milosevic through the election, despite the fact that elections in Serbia at the time were neither free nor fair.

The specific goal was to increase voter turnout, especially among traditional nonvoters, and youth in general. In theory, if these groups were to show up on election day, they would cast their ballots for the opposition candidate, bringing down the relative share of votes for Milosevic to under 50 percent. Strong voter turnout was an essential precondition to achieving the broader strategic goal, since the more of us who would show up to vote, the harder it would be to stuff ballot boxes. And the more of us who would show up to vote, the greater the outrage would be when someone tries to steal our vote.

The campaign message, as the slogan "He's Finished" clearly shows, was a message of certainty—much needed after a series of electoral defeats that left opposition voters apathetic and suspicious. Apart from posters, flyers, and the famous "He's Finished" stickers (applied to Milosevic's posters), this campaign included street theater actions.

Taking things one step further, our strategy included not only mobilizing voters but also efforts to prevent falsification of ballots. Therefore, we decided to run a parallel campaign, "Vreme Je" (It's Time). This campaign targeted more neutral voters who were interested in change but were indifferent to or turned off by the hardcore oppositional stance "He's Finished."

Unlike the "He's Finished" campaign, the "It's Time" campaign centered on rock concerts, celebrity tours, and other ways to reach less politically engaged target audiences. Also unlike the "He's Finished" campaign, which was implemented by Otpor alone, the "It's Time" campaign was conducted by a vast coalition of organizations with Otpor as one of the alliance members.

Both campaigns achieved their objectives, and with record turnout (which was up to 70 percent among voters under age 30), Milosevic lost the election.

How To Use This Book

The following several chapters contain brief introductions to explain various campaign planning tools, each accompanied by an instruction sheet and step-by-step process for using the tool in a campaign development course. Readers who will be organizing a campaign development course should begin by reading the brief introduction of a tool that precedes each instruction sheet. Once you have finished reading all tool introductions, instruction sheets, and step-by-step process explanations, check out "Campaign Development Course" on page 109 for more detailed instructions on planning such a campaign development course in the framework of a nonviolent movement.

Let's Get Started!

2. SWOT ANALYSIS: UNDERSTANDING YOUR CURRENT CAPABILITIES AND THE ENVIRONMENT

Introduction

When planning a campaign, first and foremost you need to define its objective. This objective is in the service of your vision, mission, and strategic goals, defined in your strategic plan. In other words, your strategic plan will inform you about what kinds of campaigns you should undertake. Determining the objective of each of these campaigns is part of campaign planning and requires a separate process which is informed not just by your strategic plan but also by an understanding of your current capabilities and the environment in which you're operating.

To define the campaign objective, you first need to know yourself and your environment, including your opponent. You need to understand all factors, internal as well as external, helpful as well as harmful, before you can start thinking about an objective that is realistic and relevant to your strategic goal.

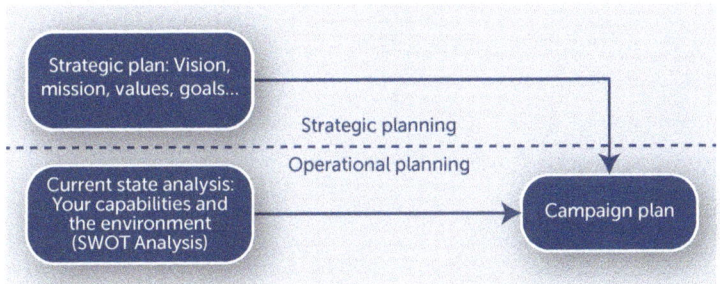

A tool that helps you identify these factors is called SWOT Analysis. SWOT is an acronym that stands for Strengths, Weaknesses, Opportunities, and Threats. It is a tool credited to Albert Humphrey from the Stanford Research Institute, although he denied he was the author. Since the 1960s, it has been used for corporate planning, but also in political campaigns and community organizing for social change.

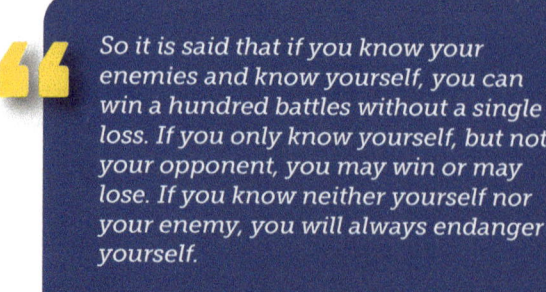

> *So it is said that if you know your enemies and know yourself, you can win a hundred battles without a single loss. If you only know yourself, but not your opponent, you may win or may lose. If you know neither yourself nor your enemy, you will always endanger yourself.*
>
> –Sun Tzu, The Art of War

Table 1: SWOT Matrix

Factors	*Helpful*	*Harmful*
Internal	**S**trengths	**W**eaknesses
External	**O**pportunities	**T**hreats

Strengths are internal capabilities such as resources (human or material), skills, or even intangible factors such as group unity or strong commitment.

Weaknesses are internal (organizational) vulnerabilities that slow you down or expose you to risks. Small numbers of activists or a lack of resources fall into this category. Factors such as lack of enthusiasm, or paralyzing fear among your fellow activists, are also considered weaknesses. Although they are less tangible than a lack of resources, they are still under your control in the sense that you can change them over time.

Opportunities are external factors that are out of your control but are beneficial to your campaign. They exist regardless of what you do. However, it is in your control to use these opportunities to your advantage during the campaign. Opportunities can be weaknesses of your opponent, including their lack of legitimacy and internal splits, but also general dissatisfaction or grievances among the population, existence of potential allies, and available resources.

Threats are also external factors that are harmful to your campaign. They are potential dangers that may never materialize. But if they do, and you haven't planned for them or do not respond properly, they may hurt your effort or even prove disastrous. Threats can include the ability of your opponent to hurt you through negative propaganda or a police crackdown, but can also cover other factors such as violent elements—external, but in physical proximity to your movement.

While conducting a SWOT Analysis, it is important to distinguish internal factors (strengths and weaknesses), which are under your control, from external factors (opportunities and threats), which exist regardless of what you do. Sometimes activists list disgruntled young people as a strength although these young people are not part of their organization, and therefore are an opportunity as potential activists—not a strength. Similarly, lack of trust among organizers and internal divisions are sometimes listed as threats to the organization, but these are actually weaknesses because they are internal to your movement.

Another thing to take into consideration is the contrast between helpful and harmful factors. While conducting a SWOT Analysis, activists rarely confuse weaknesses and strengths, but it's not so simple when it comes to external factors—threats are sometimes seen as opportunities or vice versa. For instance, repression may be seen as an opportunity, but after further analysis it turns out that the opportunity is actually the public resentment toward your opponent's repressive acts. Or, if there is no such resentment, then previous cases of repression may be an opportunity to create that public resentment. And potential repression against you during the campaign is still a threat.

In a campaign, you use opportunities and avoid threats (or mitigate their effects), but bear in mind that these factors cannot be directly created or removed. For instance, high youth unemployment may be an opportunity to mobilize young people, but mobilizing them is certainly not a given. It will be necessary to draw on organizational strengths such as an appealing campaign message and capacity to recruit additional young activists, for example through university networks. In the same line of reasoning, the threat of repression and crackdown on the campaign organizers may never materialize, but it is important to plan for it in case it does happen.

Limitations of this Tool

SWOT Analysis is not a perfect tool and has its limitations. First and foremost, not all factors are equally important. Since they are listed separately, you cannot see their interplay. This is why it is helpful to continue examining these factors with the Scenario Development Tool (explained in Chapter 3), using data gathered in the SWOT Analysis. Another limitation is that SWOT Analysis emphasizes the current state, but this can shift or change through successful implementation of a strategic plan that puts emphasis on the big picture and long-term process.

Table 2: Examples of Strengths, Weaknesses, Opportunities, and Threats

Strengths	**W**eaknesses
• Skilled and motivated team • Vision attractive to the public • Appropriate message and capacity to deliver it	• Lack of funds • Limited presence in part of the country • Internal divisions and an atmosphere of discord
Opportunities	**T**hreats
• Existence of local grassroots organizations • Spontaneous protests over food shortages • Low salaries in the government bureaucracy	• Possible arrests of campaign organizers • Biased media, negative coverage of campaign • High tensions, risk of spontaneous violence

The environment in which you implement a campaign is dynamic and changes over time, hopefully as a result of your actions. The same is true for your internal capabilities. This is why it is useful to conduct a SWOT Analysis periodically, especially before each campaign begins.

Instruction Sheet

SWOT Analysis			
Analytical	Small Group Work	No Handout	60 minutes

Quick Summary

Content	Activity	Time (min)
1. Introduce the tool	Presentation	5
2. Divide participants into four small groups	Division exercise	5
3. List factors (strengths, weaknesses, etc.)	Small group work	15
4. Report back from small groups	Group presentation and quick feedback	30
5. Conclude the exercise	Wrap-up	5
Total:		**60**

Materials Needed	When	What For
Pre-made SWOT Matrix (see endnote 1)	Presentation	Visual explanation
4 blank sheets of paper	Small group work	Listing factors
4 markers		
Adhesive tape	Wrap-up	Post lists on the wall

Before the Workshop	Before the Session
Think of an example from your experience of how SWOT Analysis helped you in your work. Turn it into a short story of up to 2-3 minutes.	Count the number of participants and decide how you are going to divide them into small groups, using lineup, scatter, or some other division exercise (see below).

Step-by-Step Process

1. Introduce the tool	Presentation	5 minutes

Start by explaining why you are doing a SWOT Analysis. Remind the participants that you are defining the campaign objective and the first step is to understand your current state—internal as well as external. This will help you take a snapshot of your current capabilities and environment. Put up the slide or a sheet of paper with the SWOT Matrix or draw one on the flip chart (a box divided into four equal sections with S, W, O, and T in each part, see image in endnote 1 on page 22).

Explain and give examples for each factor. Mark strengths and opportunities as helpful, and weaknesses and threats as harmful. Then mark strengths and weaknesses as internal, and opportunities and threats as external. Explain the difference between each pair of factors (for instance: "What is the difference between opportunities and threats? Opportunities are helpful; threats are harmful. And what is the difference between threats and weaknesses? Weaknesses are internal and threats are external."). Ask if there are any questions.

2. Divide participants into four small groups	Division exercise	5 minutes

Depending on the size of the group, you may want to use different methods to divide the participants into four small groups. Lineups are effective if the number of participants is small (less than 20 people); ask participants to line up based on their date of birth, when they usually wake up in the morning, or any other arbitrary criterion. Then walk down the line and divide it into four segments, each segment containing roughly one-quarter of the total number of participants. For larger numbers (more than 20 participants) you can scatter participants to four corners of the room by, for instance, asking people born between January and March to go to one corner, those born between April and June to another corner, and so on.

3. List factors	Small group work	15 minutes

After the division is complete, assign each small group with the task of listing their set of factors. One small group should list strengths, the second weaknesses, the third opportunities, and the fourth threats. Give each group one large sheet of paper and markers. Ask them if there are any questions, then let them know they have 15 minutes to come up with these lists and write them down on the paper they were given.

As soon as groups start working, walk around and ask each group if they need any clarification and ask them to call you if they need any help. Make another round 5 minutes later and tell them they're halfway through. Ask each small group to share with you some of the factors they have identified so far. Give them guidance if necessary, especially regarding the difference between external and internal factors. Then make another round 5 minutes later and ask each group to wrap up and finalize the list because they have only a few more minutes. Fifteen minutes into the small group work, call them back and ask them to bring their sheets of paper.

4. Report back from small groups	Presentation and quick feedback	30 minutes

Ask for a volunteer from the first group (the one that listed strengths) to come forth and quickly present their findings. After they finish, ask members of their group if they wish to add something. Then ask participants if they have any quick comments or questions, especially if they want to add a strength that isn't listed. If there are factors that you think are not strengths, ask the small group why they listed them as strengths ("Are these factors helpful? Are they internal?"). After 6-7 minutes ask the group to put their sheet of paper with listed factors on the wall and move on to the next group. Repeat the same process with each group.

Make sure to postpone any long discussion for later. Ask participants to offer only quick comments, explaining that the objective of SWOT Analysis is to list factors, while the discussion on implications and possible effects of these factors will take place later.

5. Conclude the exercise	Wrap-up	5 minutes

Thank the participants for their input and explain once again the purpose of SWOT Analysis. Give an example from your own experience of how SWOT Analysis helped you in your work. Ask if there are any final questions.

Endnotes

1. SWOT Matrix (see image on right).

2. If the number of participants is very small (less than 8 people), you may want to divide them in two groups, one listing internal factors (strengths and weaknesses) and the other external (opportunities and threats). In case of even smaller numbers (four or fewer participants), division into small groups makes no sense and the whole group should list all the factors, starting with strengths, then continuing with weaknesses, opportunities, and threats. In this case listing factors will require more time, but there will be no need for reporting and feedback.

3. SCENARIO DEVELOPMENT: ANTICIPATING POSSIBLE OUTCOMES

Introduction

To define campaign objectives, you must first understand the current state of affairs, both in terms of your internal capabilities and the environment. The objectives you develop will be based on this analysis, as well as your strategic plan. But it may be useful, before you focus on the objective, to anticipate possible developments in the near to mid-term future.

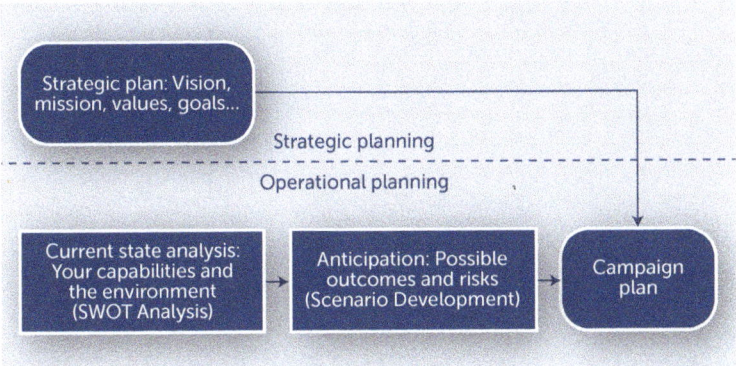

The Scenario Development Tool can be used to expand the SWOT Analysis, which gave you a snapshot of internal and external factors at a particular point in time but did not tell you much about the possible interplay of these factors in the future. To get an idea of how things may play out, you must develop scenarios using data from the SWOT Analysis.

This tool is loosely based on the TOWS Analysis developed by Heinz Weihrich from the University of San Francisco, California, USA. As a result of Scenario Development, you end up with four scenarios that may never materialize but that form boundaries within which a more realistic scenario may unfold. Scenario Development looks at the factors listed in SWOT Analysis and attempts to predict how they may together influence how things play out in the future.

Table 3: Scenario Development

	Strengths	**W**eaknesses
Opportunities	**BC** Best Case Scenario or Wishful Thinking Scenario	**MO** Missed Opportunities Scenario or Squander Scenario
Threats	**CT** Countered Threats Scenario or Mobilization Scenario	**WC** Worst Case Scenario or Nightmare Scenario

Four possible scenarios are developed using this tool: Best Case Scenario (BC), Missed Opportunities Scenario (MO), Countered Threats Scenario (CT) Comment and Worst Case Scenario (WC). Each scenario looks only at a particular pair of internal and external factors and attempts to predict what would happen if only these two sets of factors influence developments.

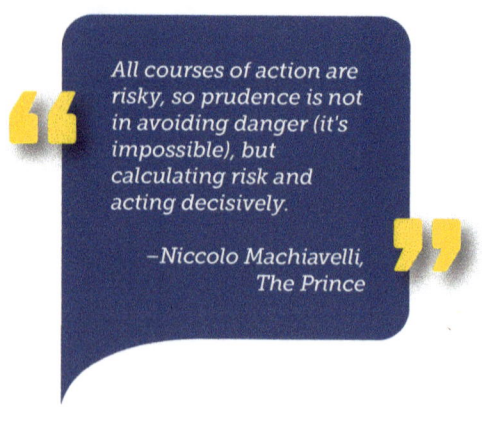

All courses of action are risky, so prudence is not in avoiding danger (it's impossible), but calculating risk and acting decisively.

—Niccolo Machiavelli, The Prince

The Best Case Scenario looks only at strengths and opportunities. It predicts developments in the event that threats never materialize and weaknesses are rather insignificant. It is unrealistic, but its purpose is to set the boundary on the positive side. This is the best you can hope for. This scenario is developed by looking at opportunities and how they can be exploited using your strengths.

The Missed Opportunities Scenario, also called the Squander Scenario, looks only at weaknesses and opportunities. It predicts developments in the event that neither threats nor strengths materialize, while the weaknesses surface. It is also unrealistic, but its purpose is to set the boundary on the negative "our fault" side. This is what you should be worried about. This scenario is developed by looking at opportunities and how they are missed or wasted because of your weaknesses.

The Countered Threats Scenario, also called the Mobilization Scenario, looks at threats and strengths. It predicts a case where there are no opportunities, just threats. However, these are met by your strengths while your weaknesses never surface. It is unrealistic as well, but sets the boundary on the positive "beating the odds" side. This is the case in which you managed to survive and triumph against all odds.

The Worst Case Scenario is developed looking at threats and weaknesses only. It's a case where there are no helpful internal or external factors—no opportunities and no strengths. It sets a boundary on the negative "no luck" side. This is the case where everything that could go wrong does go wrong—a complete catastrophe.

When developing scenarios, it is important to look only at factors that are influential under that scenario and completely disregard other factors. For instance, in the Worst Case Scenario, threats are met only with weaknesses which make the impact of these threats devastating. Repression against campaign organizers is met only by internal divisions, exaggerating the effect of the repression as a result. On the other hand, under the Countered Threats Scenario, threats are met only by strengths. Repression is met by a skilled and motivated team with an appropriate message and capacity to deliver it, which makes repression backfire.

> *The future is unwritten. There are best case scenarios. There are worst case scenarios. Both of them are great fun to write about if you're a science fiction novelist, but neither of them ever happens in the real world. What happens in the real world is always a sideways-case scenario.*
>
> *–Bruce Sterling*

Scenarios should be developed in the form of a story—a narrative that does not have to sound realistic. In fact, exaggeration is welcome because it leaves vivid images in your memory of how things could play out in extreme situations ranging from the rosy Best Case Scenario to the catastrophic Worst Case Scenario. The four scenarios help you better understand the importance of particular factors. For instance, why it's important to eliminate a particular weakness (because it amplifies the effect of some threat) or why you should focus on a certain opportunity (because you can exploit it using some of your strengths).

BC and WC scenarios are easier to develop, but with the other two there are risks. Sometimes activists can't help but see opportunities in CT scenarios or use strengths in MO scenarios. This is something you should consider when developing these scenarios. This is why it is important to understand that the MO Scenario is the "our fault" story and the CT is the "beating the odds" narrative. Below is how these two scenarios should look.

Table 4: Examples of BC, MO, CT, and WC Scenarios

	Strengths • Skilled and motivated team • Vision attractive to the public • Appropriate message and capacity to deliver it	**W**eaknesses • Lack of funds • Limited presence in parts of the country • Internal divisions and an atmosphere of discord
Opportunities • Existence of local grassroots organizations • Spontaneous protests over food shortages • Low salaries in the government bureaucracy	**BC** As a result of your campaign you form a broad-based coalition of local grassroots organizations, mobilize people over food shortages and reach out to disgruntled bureaucrats.	**MO** Your campaign gets entangled in rivalries that exist between different local organizations. You're overshadowed by spontaneous protests and you become marginalized.
Threats • Possible arrests of campaign organizers • Biased media, negative coverage of campaign • High tensions, risk of spontaneous violence	**CT** Information about arrests is shared with the population and the crackdown backfires. Your campaign survives repression and continues.	**WC** Following arrests, the campaign is in crisis because of infighting and blaming. Violence breaks out, the media blames you and your campaign falls apart.

Scenario Development has a limited purpose and should not be viewed as a predictive tool, but rather as a tool that expands your imagination of the range of possible outcomes. Scenarios developed by this tool remain in the back of your head when you continue developing your campaign and serve as boundaries within which things are more likely to happen. Since planning is not about predicting realistic outcomes, but anticipating all possible outcomes, the Scenario Development Tool helps you with this anticipation and puts you in the right place when it comes to developing a campaign plan.

In fact, there are two plans that you can build out of the stories developed by this tool. The first one is the Campaign Plan or Plan A, which details your effort to move from the MO to BC Scenario. This plan is about exploiting opportunities by using your strengths and at the same time using these opportunities to eliminate or at least reduce your weaknesses. The other plan you need to develop is the Contingency Plan or Plan B, which details your effort to move from the WC to CT Scenario. It is about using your strengths to counter threats while minimizing weaknesses.

Figure 4: Plan A and Plan B

	Strengths	Weaknesses
Opportunities	BC	MO ← PLAN A
Threats	CT	WC ← PLAN B

Plan A is your campaign plan. When you define campaign objectives, you are defining objectives for Plan A. Plan B is your contingency plan, and it is implemented only if threats listed in the SWOT Analysis begin to happen. Ideally, the only campaign you will launch will be the one outlined in Plan A, but Plan B needs to be specified beforehand because if threats materialize, there will be no time to plan a response.

Dealing with weaknesses is part of both plans, which means that reducing weaknesses is essential for capacity building with your campaign regardless of how things unfold. Although capacity building cannot be the primary objective of the campaign, the campaign can be used to build capacity of your movement or organization (recruit more people, build unity, increase funding or support, or establish a presence in a certain part of the country, for example).

After completing Scenario Development, you are ready to produce the first step of the campaign plan: campaign objectives, both for Plan A and Plan B.

Instruction Sheet

Scenario Development			
Creative	Small Group Work	Handout	90 minutes

Quick Summary

Task	Activity	Time (min)
1. Introduce the tool	Presentation	10
2. Divide participants into four small groups	Division exercise	5
3. Develop scenarios (BC, MO, CT and WC)	Small group work	15
4. Report back from small groups	Dramatization and discussion	45
5. Write down scenarios	Individual work	10
6. Finish the exercise	Wrap-up	5
Total:		**90**

Materials Needed

Materials Needed	When	What For
Pre-made sheet with Scenario Matrix	Presentation	Visual explanation
	Wrap-up	
Sticks of different lengths	Division exercise	Divide participants
SWOT & Scenario Development handout	Individual work	Writing down scenarios

Before the Workshop | Before the Session

Before the Workshop	Before the Session
	Make sure that participants have access to the factors listed in the SWOT Analysis (ideally by taping these lists to the wall of the room).

Step-by-Step Process

| 1. Introduce the tool | Presentation | 5 minutes |

Explain why you are doing Scenario Development. Remind the participants that you are defining the objective of the campaign; that you listed all the factors, internal as well as external, helpful as well as harmful, when you did the SWOT Analysis. Now you have to see how these factors may play out in the future. Put up a slide or a sheet of paper showing the Scenario Matrix or draw one on the flip chart (a box divided into four parts with the letters BC, MO, CT, and WC in each part; see endnote 1).

Explain and give examples for four scenarios: Best Case, Missed Opportunities, Countered Threats, and Worst Case Scenario (an example is provided in endnote 2). Show that different factors from the SWOT Analysis produce different scenarios (strengths and opportunities produce BC, weaknesses and opportunities MO, and so on). Explain the difference between each pair of scenarios (for instance, "What is the difference between WC and CT? In WC everything that could go wrong went wrong, including your response to threats, while in CT you managed to overcome these threats using your strengths; you managed to beat the odds."). Ask if there are any questions.

| 2. Divide participants into four small groups | Division exercise | 5 minutes |

Ask participants to divide into the same small groups they were in when they listed factors in the SWOT Analysis exercise. First go to the Strengths Group and have them draw sticks from a bunch. Send half of the group with longer sticks to one corner of the room (the BC corner) and the other to the CT corner. Then repeat the same thing with the Weaknesses Group and send half of the group to the MO corner and the other half to the WC corner. After that, go to the Opportunities Group and, based on the sticks they draw, send half of them to the BC corner and the other half to the WC corner. Finally, offer sticks to the Threats Group and send half of them to the WC corner and the other half to the CT corner. After this, you have recombined participants into four new small groups.

After the division is complete, assign each small group with the task of developing their scenario:

- The group in the BC corner should develop the Best Case Scenario looking only at strengths and opportunities, while disregarding weaknesses and threats.

- The group in the MO corner should develop the Missed Opportunities Scenario looking at opportunities and weaknesses, while ignoring strengths and threats.

- The group in the CT corner should develop the Countered Threats Scenario drawing from strengths and threats without paying attention to weaknesses and opportunities.

- The group in the WC corner should develop the Worst Case Scenario looking at weaknesses and threats, while ignoring strengths and opportunities.

Explain that the purpose of this exercise is not to develop realistic or likely scenarios but scenarios that are possible, although improbable and certainly extreme. This is in order to set boundaries within which the future may unfold. Ask participants if there are any questions and then let them know they have 15 minutes to develop scenarios and come up with a dramatization skit that they will play out in front of the whole group when you reconvene.

3. Develop scenarios (BC, MO, CT and WC)	Small group work	15 minutes

As soon as the small groups start working, walk around and ask each group if they need any clarification and ask them to call you if they need any help. Make another round 5 minutes later and let them know they are half-way through. Ask each small group about their progress and offer them guidance if necessary. Then make another round 5 minutes later and ask each group to wrap up and finalize the list because they have only a few more minutes. Fifteen minutes into the small group work, call them back.

4. Report back from small groups	Dramatization and discussion	45 minutes

Explain to participants that you will now dramatize each scenario and discuss them, starting with the Missed Opportunities Scenario, followed by the Best Case Scenario. Then you will have a short discussion after which you will play out and discuss the remaining two scenarios.

Ask the members of the MO group to take the stage and play out their skit. After they finish, ask members of the BC group to perform their skit. When the BC group is done, ask participants how they liked the two skits and if they have any thoughts about what they just saw. Ask what the main differences were between two scenarios. Why was the BC group able to exploit opportunities? What were the biggest weaknesses in the MO group? End the discussion after 20 minutes.

Now ask members of the WC group to play out their dramatization of the Worst Case Scenario. After they finish, ask the CT group to take the stage and perform. After they finish ask participants to share their thoughts about these two skits. Ask about the main differences between the scenarios. Why was the CT group able to counter threats? Why were threats so devastating in the WC group? Use the remaining time allocated to this activity for discussion.

| 5. Write down scenarios | Individual work | 10 minutes |

Distribute SWOT and Scenario Handouts to participants and ask them to write down factors from the lists posted on the wall of the room, and then to describe in writing the four scenarios they have just seen played out. Explain that you will use this information later when you start defining campaign objectives.

| 6. Conclude the exercise | Wrap-up | 5 minutes |

Thank the participants for their skits and show them once again the Scenario Matrix. Draw two arrows, one from MO to BC labeled "Plan A" and the other from WC to CT labeled "Plan B." Explain that you are now ready to develop two campaign plans: Plan A and Plan B. Plan A will move you away from the Missed Opportunities Scenario toward the Best Case Scenario. Your second and contingency plan, Plan B, is what you move to if Plan A is not working. This plan moves you away from the Worst Case Scenario toward the Countered Threats Scenario. Ask if there are any final questions and get started.

Endnotes

1. Scenario Matrix (see image on page 34).

2. Example of BC, MO, CT and WC Scenarios:

> Let's say we have a guy who wants to marry a girl. His strength is that he is charming and handsome, but his weakness is that he is broke. An opportunity is that the girl is in love with him, but the threat is that her parents would like to see their daughter marry someone who has plenty of money....The Best Case Scenario is that he's charming and good looking and she's in love with him, so they get married. The Missed Opportunities Scenario is that she's

in love with him, but he is broke so he does not dare to propose, but rather looks for a job. The Countered Threats Scenario is that he's charming and handsome and manages to charm her parents, so they do not oppose the marriage. The Worst Case Scenario is he is broke and her parents persuade their daughter that she should look for a better match. As you can see, in the BC and MO scenarios you don't care about the girl's parents, and in the CT and WC scenarios you don't care about the girl. In the BC and CT scenarios you don't care that the guy is broke, while in the WC and MO scenarios you don't care that the guy is charming and handsome. All these scenarios are improbable, but they define the boundaries within which a more realistic scenario will take place.

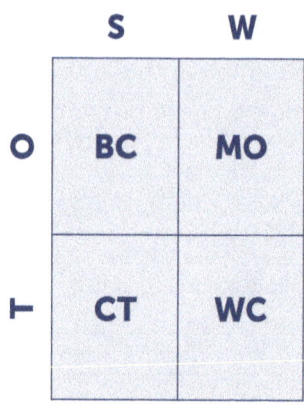

4. SMART CRITERIA: SETTING CAMPAIGN OBJECTIVES

Introduction

The first element of the campaign plan is the campaign objective. It answers the question, "What do you want to achieve with your campaign?" Campaign objectives are informed by your strategic plan, your analysis of the current situation, your capabilities, and the environment in which you operate. Good campaign objectives advance your long-term strategy, as laid out in your strategic plan. They also take into account all the internal and external factors, helpful as well as harmful (which you understood using SWOT Analysis). Good campaign objectives can also be tested against all possible developments in the future—ranging from best case to worst case scenario—which can arise as an interplay of these different factors and which you also should be able to anticipate (using Scenario Development).

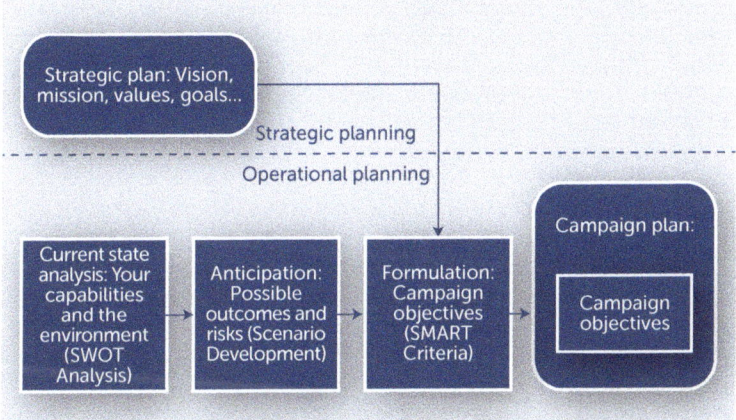

In coming up with campaign objectives, you can use SMART criteria to come up with SMART objectives. SMART is an acronym first used by George T. Doran in 1981, and SMART criteria are commonly attributed to Peter Drucker's management by objectives concept. Different criteria have been associated with these letters over the years, but the most common use of the letters in the acronym is as follows:

S - specific
M - measurable
A - achievable
R - relevant
T - time-bound

The criterion "specific" stresses the need for concrete rather than vague objectives. Specific objectives are about changing behavior rather than opinion. Raising awareness and pushing for reform are examples of unclear objectives. Obtaining 10,000 signatures on a petition or getting a bill introduced in parliament are examples of specific objectives.

The second criterion points you to the importance of measurement. Objectives you can measure after the campaign ends are important for building a winning record. It is also important to be able to measure progress. For some campaigns this is possible (for instance if you run a petition drive, you can easily measure its progress along the way), while for others you can only conduct measurements after the campaign has ended (election campaigns are a good example of this). But even in these cases, you should find ways to measure your progress and make necessary adjustments to your campaign if needed.

Objectives also need to be achievable rather than unrealistic. This means that the objective should be chosen after careful analysis of your capabilities, the environment, and most importantly, your strengths as helpful internal factors that you can control. Persuading people to support and join your effort will largely depend on this criterion. Building a winning record is best done through small victories (achievable and eventually achieved objectives).

We say that an objective is relevant if it relates to the long-term goal laid out in your strategic plan and if you can see how this objective is in service to your long-term strategy. This criterion helps you keep all your campaigns within your strategic framework so you know why you are implementing a particular campaign. Most people will not read your mission statement, but they will be exposed to it through your actions within a campaign. Therefore, they should be able to see and understand your strategy through your campaigns. This is why there has to be a clear connection between campaign objectives and strategic goals.

Time-bound objectives specify how and when the campaign is going to end. Campaigns should not be open-ended; they should have a start and end organized around a clear timeframe. This is true even if the objectives are not achieved or you do not produce the results you'd hoped for. Once the campaign ends, you can measure its success. Campaigns seldom completely fail or completely succeed, which allows you to see what worked and what didn't work—teaching you lessons for future campaigns.

SMART Criteria Example: Gandhi's Salt March

One of the most important campaigns in the Indian nonviolent struggle for independence from British rule was the Salt March. Gandhi wrote a letter to the Viceroy shortly before starting a 380 km journey on foot to the Indian Ocean to make salt and thus break the Salt Laws. In this letter he stated the objective of the campaign, which challenged the British monopoly on salt and ultimately the British rule over India:

> *"If my letter makes no appeal to your heart, on the eleventh day of this month I shall proceed with such co-workers of the Ashram as I can take, to disregard the provisions of the Salt Laws. I regard this tax to be the most iniquitous of all from the poor man's standpoint. As the sovereignty and self-rule movement is essentially for the poorest in the land, the beginning will be made with this evil."*

- Gandhi's letter to the Viceroy, Lord Irwin on March 2, 1930

Let's analyze Gandhi's Salt March using SMART criteria.

Specific	"... to disregard the provisions of the Salt Laws."
Measurable	"I shall proceed [...] to disregard the provisions..."
Achievable	"I shall proceed with such co-workers of the Ashram as I can take..."
Relevant	"I regard this tax to be the most iniquitous of all from the poor man's standpoint. As the sovereignty and self-rule movement is essentially for the poorest in the land, the beginning will be made with this evil."
Time-bound	"... on the eleventh day of this month I shall proceed..."

It is important to note the difference between the objective and the effect of the Salt March campaign. Gandhi undertook civil disobedience and broke the Salt Laws at 6:30 am on April 6, 1930, which meant that the specific objective of the campaign was achieved. By itself, this was rather symbolic. However, the campaign had a significant and broad effect on changing people's attitudes toward Indian sovereignty and led large numbers of Indians to join the fight for independence.

After using SWOT Analysis and Scenario Development in your operational planning process, you can use SMART criteria to come up with objectives for your campaign plan (Plan A) and your contingency plan (Plan B).

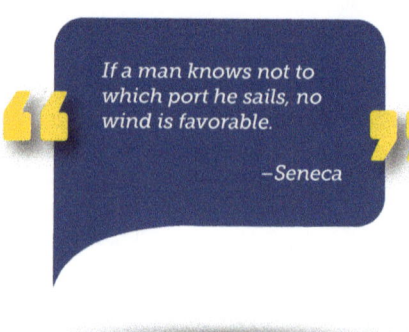

If a man knows not to which port he sails, no wind is favorable.

–Seneca

The Plan A objective is specific if it exploits concrete opportunities to move you further away from the MO Scenario toward the BC Scenario. It is measurable if you can assess and measure how these opportunities were used. It is also measurable if you can compare your weaknesses before the start of the campaign and after its end and determine if some of the weaknesses were reduced or completely removed.

The Plan B objective is specific if it recognizes and counters concrete threats to move you further away from the WC Scenario toward the CT Scenario. It is measurable if you can measure how these threats were reduced—especially if you can measure your weaknesses and determine whether they were worsened by these threats.

Both Plan A and Plan B objectives are achievable if they use your realistic strengths, because your strengths are positive factors within your control. They are relevant if they relate to your strategic goals. They are time-bound if the campaign has a beginning and an end, either in absolute terms (exact dates) or in relative terms (in relation to external events or other campaigns you are planning).

Side note: One can potentially use SMART criteria when defining strategic goals, but this is not the best use for this tool, since a strategic plan is broad and wide-reaching—and thus does not include specific goals. Measuring outcomes for a strategic plan is also problematic since strategy takes years to implement. You can measure progress more easily than results. Strategic goals don't always look achievable, at least at the outset, because the capacity required to reach them will be built over time as the strategy slowly unfolds. It is also difficult to envision a time-bound, long-term goal, since such a distant future is not very time-bound and could take five years, 10 years, or longer to achieve. But strategic goals can and should still be relevant—they should relate to your vision, mission, and values.

Instruction Sheet

Smart Criteria			
Analytical	Individual Work	Handout	30 minutes

Quick Summary

Task	Activity	Time (min)
1. Introduce the tool	Presentation	10
2. Write down objectives	Individual work (using SMART handout)	15
3. Conclude the exercise	Wrap-up	5
Total:		**30**

Materials Needed	When	What For
Pre-made flip chart with listed SMART criteria	Presentation	Visual explanation
Excerpt from Gandhi's letter	Presentation	Example
SMART handouts	Individual work	Writing objectives
Pens	Individual work	Writing objectives

Before the Workshop	Before the Session
Write the excerpt from Gandhi's letter to Lord Irwin on a large sheet of paper (see endnote 1).	Make sure participants have access to the list of broad aims (ideally by posting them on wall of the room).

Step-by-Step Process

| 1. Introduce the tool | Presentation | 10 minutes |

Explain the purpose of SMART criteria to guide you in setting objectives that are clear and understandable. Display the sheet of paper with listed criteria and explain, giving examples for each letter in the acronym.

Display the excerpt from Gandhi's letter on the flip chart or on the wall behind you (see endnote 1). Describe briefly the Salt March campaign and tell participants that you will now look at the letter Gandhi wrote to Lord Irwin. Read aloud the excerpt which lays out the objective of the campaign.

Ask participants if this objective is specific. Ask them to read that part of the text. Ask if it is measurable. Ask if it is achievable. If they say yes, ask why. Ask how it is relevant. Ask if it is time-bound. Underline each segment of the letter that meets a criterion. Then let participants know that they are going to make their own SMART objectives.

| 2. Write down objectives | Individual work | 15 minutes |

Distribute SMART handouts. Ask participants to pick an aim and rewrite it into an objective by answering questions listed on the handout (what, when, how, and why). Give them a few minutes to complete the task. Then ask them to pass the handout to the person on their right and continue passing handouts they receive (from the person on their left) to the person on their right until you say stop.

After you say stop, ask participants to read the objective they have in their hands and check appropriate boxes in the distributed handouts if they think that objective meets any of the SMART criteria. Ask them to offer suggestions on how to improve the objective in the handout if they have not checked all the boxes or if they have fresh ideas.

Give them a few minutes then ask them to pass the handout to the person on their right and keep on passing them until they end up with their original handout.

Tell participants to make adjustments to their objectives if necessary, based on the suggestions they have received.

| 3. Finish the exercise | Discussion | 5 minutes |

Ask participants if there are any objectives that have not met SMART criteria. If there are any, then offer suggestions on how to improve them. Ask if there are any final questions.

Endnotes

1. Excerpt from Gandhi's letter to Lord Irwin:

   "If my letter makes no appeal to your heart, on the eleventh day of this month I shall proceed with such co-workers of the Ashram as I can take, to disregard the provisions of the Salt Laws. I regard this tax to be the most iniquitous of all from the poor man's standpoint. As the sovereignty and self-rule movement is essentially for the poorest in the land, the beginning will be made with this evil."

   - Gandhi's letter to the Viceroy, Lord Irwin on March 2, 1930

2. The handout with SMART criteria looks like this:

   Campaign Objective

   What do we want to do?

   When do we want to do it?

   Why do we want to do it?

   How are we going to do it?

Specific?	☐
Measurable?	☐
Achievable?	☐
Relevant?	☐
Time-bound?	☐

5. SPECTRUM OF ALLIES: MAPPING STAKEHOLDERS

Introduction

Message is central to a campaign. It can be said that the whole campaign is developed for the purpose of conveying the campaign message. All the tactics, all the activities in the campaign, all its materials carry that same message reinforced again and again, tailored to specific targeted audiences. The message aims to ultimately change people's behavior, not just their perceptions and beliefs. This is why campaigns must continue for longer periods of time (usually months) to allow the message to sink in and create change.

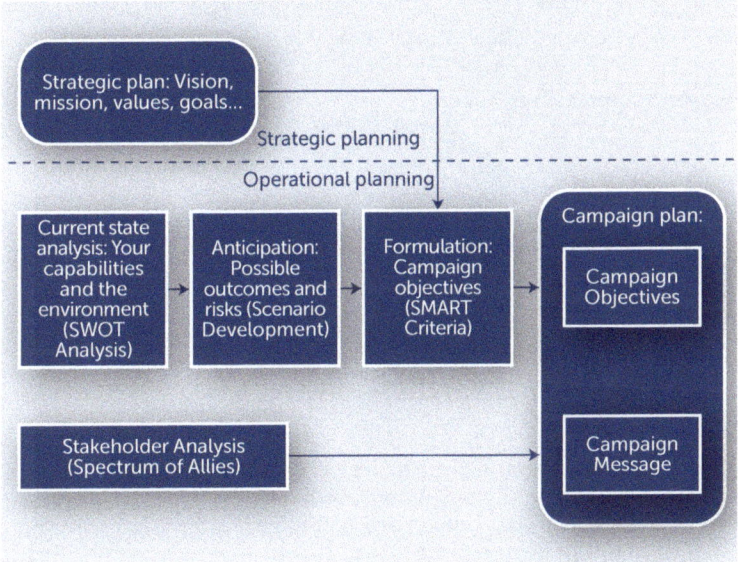

When crafting the campaign message, you must first define target audiences—recipients of that message. Your campaign cannot reach and affect everyone in society so you need to clearly define who is in one way or another connected to the campaign issue, whether they are supportive of your position on that issue or not. For instance, if the campaign issue is education, the audience would be students, teachers, and administrators, but also students' parents. If it is land reform, you would look at farmers, landless peasants, and landowners, but also farm workers and other groups connected directly or indirectly to agriculture.

Take any issue and survey the segment of the population broadly enough, and you will find that not all people have the same position on that issue—some support it, some oppose it, some are neutral. Even within each segment of the population, not all people support or oppose something with the same level of conviction and enthusiasm. This is why the message of the campaign must be carefully tailored for each target audience so it corresponds to their perceptions, is relevant to their situation, creates interest and engagement, and leads to desired changes in their behavior.

A tool that helps you differentiate between various target audiences is called the Spectrum of Allies (see Figure 5). Developed by George Lakey and Martin Oppenheimer of Training for Change almost half a century ago, it encapsulates the notion that the target of your campaign is not monolithic, but segmented and spread across a spectrum. As a result, your campaign message should consist of a number of sub-messages, each tailored for a particular target audience.

Figure 5: Spectrum of Allies

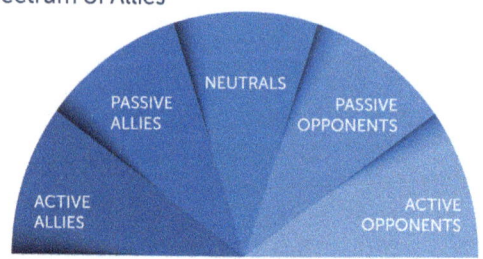

Source: Training for Change

If you use the Spectrum to define your target audiences, you can categorize them into several segments. On the far-left side of the spectrum are so-called active allies, individuals and groups who share your position on the campaign issue and are willing to do something about it (offer assistance or resources, endorse your campaign, get involved or help in some other way). These are the people who are already actively involved and whom your campaign can count on.

In the next segment are so-called passive allies, individuals and groups supporting your campaign passively, or just sharing your position on the issue without knowing that there is a campaign tackling it. These are people your campaign could turn into active allies with the least amount of effort, since they are already convinced of the validity of your position—they just haven't gotten involved yet.

The central segment, and in most cases the largest, are people who are neutral—they neither support nor oppose your position on the issue. They are either unaware or apathetic, and either way, they are not mobilized, neither by you nor by your opponents.

The segment right-of-center consists of individuals and groups who are opposed to you and your campaign but remain passive about it. They do not engage in any activity that undermines your efforts, but these people are not on your side and do not agree with your position, even if their resolve is not very strong. They are called passive opponents.

The far-right segment of the spectrum is so-called active opponents, individuals and groups doing everything they can to undermine your effort. These people are on the other side of the issue actively attempting to fight your position and your efforts.

> ### Case Study: U.S. Civil Rights Movement
>
> In 1964, the Student Nonviolent Coordinating Committee (SNCC), a major driver of the civil rights movement in the U.S. South, conducted a "spectrum-of-allies style" analysis. They determined that they had a lot of passive allies who were students in the North: these students were sympathetic, but had no entry point into the movement. They didn't need to be "educated" or convinced, they needed an invitation to enter.
>
> To shift these allies from "passive" to "active," SNCC sent buses north to bring folks down to participate in the struggle under the banner "Freedom Summer." Students came in droves, and many were deeply radicalized in the process, witnessing lynching, violent police abuse, and angry white mobs, all simply as a result of black activists trying to vote.
>
> Many wrote letters home to their parents, who suddenly had a personal connection to the struggle. This triggered another shift: their families became passive allies, often bringing their workplaces and social networks with them. The students, meanwhile, went back to school in the fall and proceeded to organize their campuses. More shifts. The result: a profound transformation of the political landscape of the U.S. This cascading shift of support, it's important to emphasize, wasn't spontaneous; it was part of a deliberate movement strategy that, to this day, carries profound lessons for other movements.
>
> (Joshua Kahn Russell, "Spectrum of Allies," *Beautiful Trouble*)

The idea behind the Spectrum of Allies is to identify all the relevant stakeholders and place them on the spectrum based on their position on the issue and their willingness to fight for their position. Your campaign must have a very specific effect on these people—to move them at least one step closer to your position (i.e., one step to the left). In other words, your goal is not to turn active opponents into active allies (not even to turn passive opponents or neutrals to active allies), but to move them just one step to their left on the spectrum. You must turn active opponents into passive opponents, passive opponents into neutrals, neutrals into passive allies and finally passive allies into active allies. You should be aware that your opponents aren't stagnant and will be working to move groups the opposite way.

By achieving a slight move to the left for many segments of the population, you will have a significant impact on the overall repositioning of stakeholders. The behavioral changes you seek to induce are fairly small and therefore realistic. You do not need to convince your active opponents that they are wrong. They can still continue to hold their beliefs, but you are trying to undermine their determined position against you. Your passive opponents do not need to change their minds completely by abandoning their views and accepting yours; weakening their positions and becoming neutral will be enough. As for the neutrals, they do not need to take an active role in your campaign. You just need to make them more sympathetic to your cause. Active support and engagement is what you want from passive allies, those who are already convinced that your position on the issue is the correct one.

When using the Spectrum of Allies, it is important to list all the relevant stakeholders first before putting them on the spectrum. Active allies and active opponents are the easiest to identify, but careful analysis will reveal other groups and individuals, currently on the margins of the conflict around a given issue. These people may prove crucial to swaying the pendulum to your side by creating a critical mass that is no longer silent on the issue—that is, mobilized around it and creating additional pressure on those opposing you to give up or give in.

Another important thing to remember is that you want to create gradual, incremental changes in behavior of people your campaign is targeting. In that sense, you are not interested so much in your active opponents, except that you want to reduce their enthusiasm and willingness to fight. You are most interested in influencing the segments of the spectrum in the middle—neutrals as well as passive allies and passive opponents.

But for each segment the desired behavioral change is slightly different, and your message needs to reflect that. The desired behavioral change for passive allies is to make them more active (i.e., involved in your campaign), for neutrals to make them sympathetic, and for passive opponents to make them doubt their position on the issue. Even within each segment, groups may need different types of message delivery. An example is neutral youth versus neutral retirees.

If there is one tool that most dramatically unveils the dynamics of civil resistance, it would be the Spectrum of Allies. It shows both the varying levels of support that different groups have and the gradual shifting of loyalties—one step to the left—that is the objective of a nonviolent struggle. This is why, apart from being used as a tool to develop a campaign message, the Spectrum of Allies can be used to introduce civil resistance as a method more broadly.

Instruction Sheet

Spectrum of Allies			
Analytical	Group Work	Handout	30 minutes

Content

Task	Activity	Time (min)
1. Introduce the tool	Presentation	5
2. List stakeholders	Group work	10
3. Position stakeholders on the spectrum	Group work	10
4. Finish the exercise	Wrap-up	5
Total:		30

Materials Needed	When	What For
Sticky notes	Group work	Listing stakeholders
Pre-made Spectrum of Allies (see endnote 1)	Group work	Positioning stakeholders

Before the Workshop	Before the Session
	Provide access to campaign objective, ideally by posting it on the wall of the room

Step-by-Step Process

| 1. Introduce the tool | Presentation | 5 minutes |

Start by explaining the reason for using the Spectrum of Allies. Remind participants that you already have the campaign objective but still need to craft the campaign message. The first step in message development is to clearly define target audiences, and this tool will help you do this.

Display the pre-made sheet with the Spectrum or draw one on the whiteboard. Explain and give examples for each segment on the spectrum. Explain the difference between active and passive allies, and active and passive opponents. Explain the neutral segment on the spectrum. Ask if there are any questions.

| 2. List stakeholders | Group work | 10 minutes |

Distribute sticky notes to participants and ask them to take out their pens. Prompt participants to think of a group, formal or informal, that is in some way connected to the issue on which your campaign focuses. Ask participants to write down the name of the group on the sticky note. Ask participants to call out groups from their sticky notes. Explain that if they hear the name of the group they thought of called out by someone else, they should try to think of another group and write it down.

| 3. Position stakeholders | Group work | 10 minutes |

Ask participants to stand up, one by one, and approach the Spectrum sheet to post their sticky note on the appropriate segment of the spectrum. Ask participants if they agree with the positioning of that group. Briefly discuss if there are disagreements and move on to the next participant. Note that sometimes a group will be divided and placed in one or two different segments such as "progressive press," "mainstream press," and "government-run press," or "fundamentalist Christians" and "liberation-theology Christians." It's important to capture these differences within broad categories of the population. After all the sticky notes have been posted, ask participants if all the segments were populated and if there are any other groups that should be on the spectrum.

| 4. End the exercise | Wrap-up | 5 minutes |

Thank the participants for their input and explain once again the purpose of the Spectrum of Allies. Ask if there are any final questions.

Endnotes

The Spectrum of Allies (see image below).

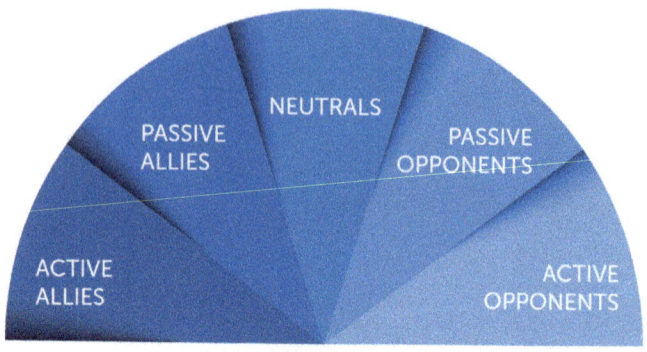

6. PERCEPTION BOX: ANALYZING STAKEHOLDERS' BELIEFS AND FEELINGS

Introduction

Messaging is central to your campaign, and if crafted carefully it will have a greater impact. This is why understanding the target audiences is crucial for campaign success. Once you have defined different stakeholders and positioned them on the Spectrum of Allies, you can analyze their perceptions to better inform your message development process and produce the optimal message. Messages need to be carefully tailored for each target audience, and understanding audience perceptions is key to designing a message that will resonate with them. In other words, you must know who you are talking to and where they are coming from with regard to the campaign issue. This will allow you to tell them something that will move them toward you.

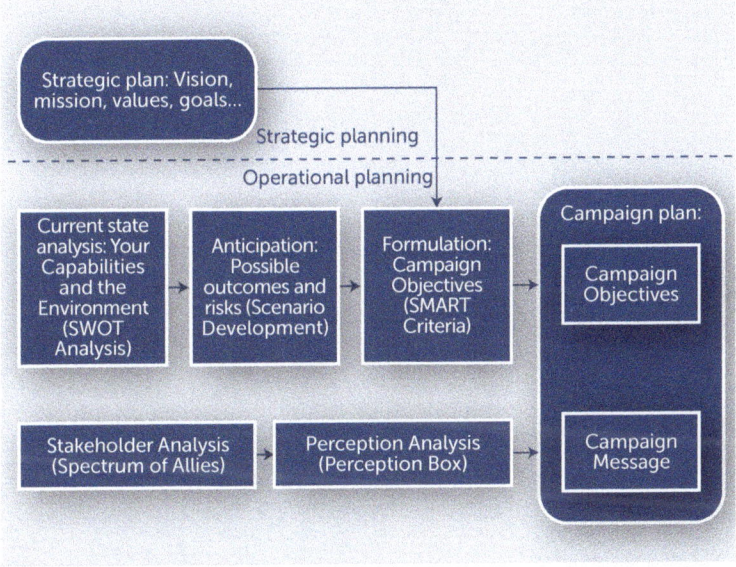

A tool that helps you understand these perceptions is called the Perception Box. The version used here is a modification of the original Tully Message Box (named after political strategist Paul Tully), which is often used in election campaigns. The original Message Box is used to craft a message that will help a candidate stand out among other candidates. The modified version presented here, called Perception Box, looks not only at your active opponents in elections but at every segment you defined in the Spectrum of Allies.

The Perception Box has four quadrants. The first quadrant, titled "We about Us," lists all the things you say about yourselves and your campaign. It reflects both your strategic communication elements—

your identity as an organization/coalition/movement (your brand)—and your assertions related to the campaign you are launching. It lists who you are, what you want, and why. Not only does it specify your broad vision (your ends) and mission (your means) but it specifies your grievances and demands.

The second quadrant, named "Us about Them," lists your perception of the given target audiences. When you define the Perception Box for your Passive and Active Opponents, you fill this quadrant in with your perception of them, like in Tully's Message Box. But when you develop the Perception Box for Neutrals or Passive Allies, you list your perceptions of that particular target audience, including misconceptions you may have about them.

We about Us	Us about Them
They about Us	They about Them

The third quadrant, titled "They about Us" lists perceptions that particular target audiences have about you and your campaign, including misconceptions. When defining this quadrant for Neutrals or Passive or Active Opponents, you should list all the reservations they have about you. When defining it for Passive Allies, you should see inhibitions and reasons for the lack of their active involvement in the campaign.

In the fourth and final quadrant, "They about Them," you list perceptions of the target audience about themselves, in particular the reasons why they occupy their particular segment on the spectrum. For Neutrals you want to know why they are neutral on the issue, whether or not they are aware of it, whether or not they are apathetic, and so on. For Opponents, both Active and Passive, you must figure out why they hold the beliefs they do, and the reason for their stance on the issue in question. For Passive Allies you want to figure out why they remain inactive despite the fact that they have the same position on the issue as you do.

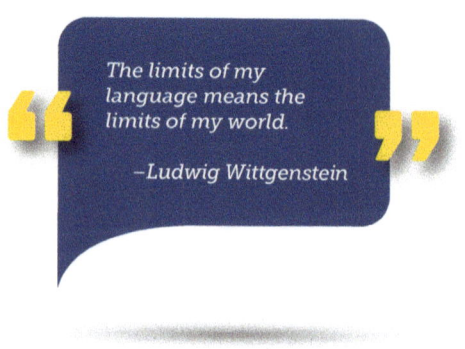

The limits of my language means the limits of my world.

–Ludwig Wittgenstein

Note: To simplify the analysis and fit it into a workshop, you can imagine what others are feeling and use any information you have about them. To develop a more robust set of information, you can use questionnaires, polling, or even focus groups with the segments of the population you are analyzing to get feedback directly from them in their words.

Once these perceptions are listed, discussed, and finalized, you can use the Perception Box to bridge the divide between you and the given target audience through the message you are about to craft. Analysis of the target audience and its perceptions set the groundwork for message development. It gives you information for crafting the campaign message, which must meet certain criteria:

- The message should be clear. It should state both the problem and the proposition or "ask" to the target audience with clarity and in relatively simple terms.

- The message should be catchy, to grab the attention of the target audience and leave a lasting impression.

- And finally, the message should create behavioral change—to ultimately move the target one step to the left on the Spectrum of Allies.

Your message for a particular audience consists of two parts:

- The first part of the message states the campaign issue through the target's "They about Them" perception lens, avoiding and even countering your misconceptions about the target listed in the "Us about Them" quadrant.

- The second part connects your campaign to the target using your "We about Us" and countering "They about Us" misconceptions.

The first part of the message states the problem not just from your angle but also from the angle of the target audience. For example, if the campaign issue is police brutality and the target audience is police officers, you must state the problem not as a violation of your human rights, but as a misuse of the police force which officers joined to fight crime, not to quell democratic dissent and beat innocent people.

The second part contains your proposition or "ask" to the target audience. What do you want them to do or stop doing? In the above example, the proposition to the officers is to refrain from using force against activists. This proposition is backed by connecting the fact that you are peaceful protesters and that their desire is to maintain peace and stability.

Perception Box Example: Police Brutality	
We about Us: • We are peaceful protesters • Our human rights must be respected • We are not doing anything illegal when we protest	**Us about Them:** • The police are brutal and unaccountable • The police are not doing their job—fighting crime—but instead quelling peaceful dissent • The police are the regime's praetorian guard
They about Us: • Protesters are disruptive and unruly • Protesters make our work more difficult • Protesters should use legal channels to voice their grievances	**They about Them:** • We protect the people and maintain peace • We fight crime and prevent disorder but never get credit for that • We are just following orders
Message (Talking Points): • We want the police to protect the people, maintain peace, fight crime and prevent disorder • We know the police to want the same thing and they should be allowed to focus on that, not to be misused against people with legitimate political or societal grievances • The problem is not the police, but the orders given to police • We are peaceful protesters and peaceful protest is a legal channel to voice our grievances and demands • We should work together to maintain peace and prevent disorder; it's our common goal	

At this stage, the campaign message takes the form of talking points—statements that either stand alone or in opposition to claims made by the adversary and with the purpose of refuting them. They are condensed and succinct, often in the form of short phrases or single sentences, and sometimes presented as bullet points. These talking points cannot be used in campaign material directly but serve as a basis for your communication with the public as the campaign unfolds. You use these talking points to develop slogans, visuals and soundbites. You use them when you develop tactics, write articles, or give speeches.

The Perception Box is an analytical tool that gives you enough information to begin the creative part of message development.

However, a well-defined Perception Box does not guarantee the success of the campaign and its message. This still depends on the creativity invested in slogans, tactics, campaign materials, and dissemination of the message. But a poorly defined Perception Box cannot produce the optimal message, despite all the creativity you may employ in later stages of planning.

Instruction Sheet

Perception Box			
Analytical	Group Work	Handout	30 minutes

Quick Summary

Content	Activity	Time (min)
1. Introduce the tool	Presentation	5
2. Divide participants into four small groups	Division exercise	5
3. List perceptions (WaU, WaT, TaU, TaT)	Small group work	15
4. Report back from small groups	Presentation and discussion	30
5. Finish the exercise	Wrap-up	5
Total:		**60**

Materials Needed	When	What For
Pre-made sheet with Spectrum of Allies	Presentation	Visual explanation
	Wrap-up	
Marbles of different colors	Division exercise	Divide participants
Large sheets of paper	Small group work	Create Perception Boxes
Markers		

Before the Workshop	Before the Session
Marbles or other small objects in five different colors, one for each participant. Each color should be around one-fifth of the total number of objects.	Make sure that participants have access to target audiences shown on the Spectrum of Allies (ideally by taping the Spectrum to the wall of the room).

Step-by-Step Process

| 1. Introduce the tool | Presentation | 5 minutes |

Explain why you are creating the Perception Box. Show different stakeholders on the Spectrum of Allies and explain that each group has a different perception of you and your campaign, and that you need to understand these perceptions if you want to craft an adequate message that will resonate with each of these groups. Explain that you need to know not only what they think about you and your campaign, but also what they think about themselves. At the same time, you must state what you think about yourselves and specify your current perception of them. This should be done for every group on the Spectrum.

| 2. Divide participants into five small groups | Division exercise | 5 minutes |

Ask participants to draw marbles and assign each color to a particular segment on the Spectrum of Allies—one is Active Allies, the other is Passive Allies, and so on. Ask participants to form small groups based on the color of the marbles they drew. After the division is complete, assign each small group with the task of listing perceptions of the groups in their respective segments of the Spectrum and in the four quadrants of the Perception Box. They should list "We about Us"—perceptions you have about yourselves; "Us about Them"—perceptions you have of the target; "They about Us"—the target's perceptions about you; and "They about Them"—the target's perception of themselves. Give them large sheets of paper (one for each small group) and markers. Ask them if there are any questions and let them know they have 15 minutes to come up with these lists on the paper they were given.

| 3. List perceptions (WaU, UaT, TaU, TaT) | Small group work | 15 minutes |

As soon as the small groups start working, walk around and ask each group if they need any clarification. Ask them to call you if they need any help. Make another round 5 minutes later and let them know they are half-way through. Ask each small group if they need help and give them guidance if necessary. Then make another round 5 minutes later and ask each group to wrap up and finalize the list because they have only a few more minutes. Fifteen minutes into the small group work ask them to finish and call them back.

| 4. Report back from small groups | Presentation and discussion | 30 minutes |

Explain to participants that you will now discuss Perception Boxes for each segment of the Spectrum, and that you will start with Active Allies, followed by Passive Allies. Then you will have a short discussion, after which you will present and discuss Perception Boxes for Active and Passive Opponents. Finally, you will present and discuss the Perception Box for Neutrals.

Ask the members of the Active Allies small group to take the stage and present their Perception Box. After they finish, ask members of the Passive Allies small group to present their Perception Box. After they finish, ask participants if they have any thoughts about the two Perception Boxes. Ask what the main differences between Active and Passive Allies are. What do they have in common, apart from sharing the same position on the campaign issue? How could you turn Passive Allies into Active Allies? After 10 minutes move on to the next two small groups.

Ask the members of the Active Opponents small group to present their Perception Box. After they finish, ask members of the Passive Opponents small group to present their Perception Box. After they finish ask participants for comments and suggestions. Ask what the main differences between Active and Passive Opponents are. What do they have in common, apart from sharing the same position on the campaign issue? How could you turn Active Opponents into Passive Opponents? After 10 minutes move on to the last small group.

Ask the Neutral small group to present their Perception Box. After they finish their presentation, ask participants to comment and offer suggestions. Ask what the main differences between Passive Allies and Neutrals are, and also what they have in common. Ask the same about Passive Opponents and Neutrals. Ask how you could turn Neutrals into Passive Allies and Passive Opponents into Neutrals. After 10 minutes conclude the discussion.

| 5. Conclude the exercise | Wrap-up | 5 minutes |

Thank the participants for their presentations and show the Spectrum of Allies one last time. Explain that you need to move each group one position to the left and use the Perception Box to come up with the right message for each group. The message must be built on their perceptions about themselves and work to bridge these perceptions with your perception of yourselves and your campaign, countering misconceptions they have about you and that you have about them. Ask if there are any final questions.

Endnotes

1. Perception Box (see image below).

We about Us	Us about Them
They about Us	They about Them

7. BRAINSTORMING: CONJURING UP TACTICS

Introduction

Finally, after all the analytical work put into crafting a message, the creative part of campaign development can begin. A message developed by using the Perception Box and presented in the form of talking points is not suitable for distribution. It must be condensed and modified so it can be spread through different means: campaign material, tactics, articles, speeches, social media, and so on. The creation of talking points thus must be followed by group discussion on the ways your message can be conveyed to the respective target audiences.

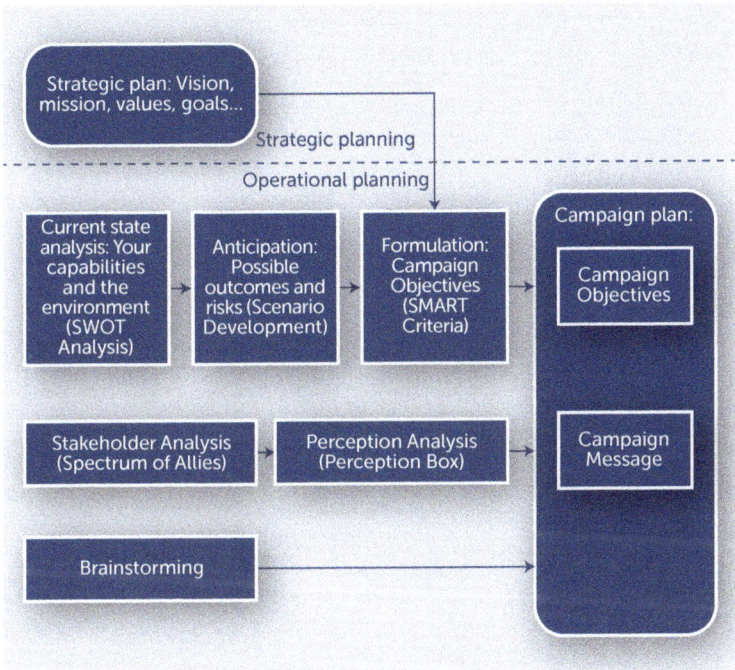

A tool that can help you in this creative process is called Brainstorming. The term was popularized by Alex Faickney Osborn in his book *Applied Imagination* published in 1953. Osborn defined two principles for successful brainstorming:

– Defer judgment

– Reach for quantity

The reason for deferring judgment is to enable ideas to be generated. Participants in a brainstorm are discouraged from judging others' or their own ideas for two main reasons. First, judgment shifts the focus to the ideas already generated, rather than on potential new ones. Second, judgment may discourage some people from offering novel and unorthodox propositions, believing that these would be met with harsh criticism or even ridicule. There is no room for critiquing during a brainstorming session; it should be left for later. Instead, creativity and connections should be encouraged and people should expand on each others' ideas.

Osborn says we should aim to produce as many ideas as possible since, in his view, quantity will later lead to quality. You will have a larger pool of ideas from which to pick the best ones. Osborn thus believed that during brainstorming sessions, you need to reduce people's inhibitions, stimulate idea generation, and increase the overall creativity of the group.

Osborn noted that brainstorming should address a specific question. He believed that sessions addressing multiple questions were inefficient. This is why brainstorming works best if it follows careful analysis of stakeholders, their perceptions, and the message to those stakeholders presented in the form of talking points. Brainstorming should thus be used to look at each item in the talking points separately.

Ideas produced during brainstorming can take any form or direction and they can change as the session progresses. They can morph or split. Slogans can become tactics, tactics can turn into posters, posters can become videos, and so on. The ideas themselves can branch out from an initial idea, proposed by one participant, to several mutated versions or variations of the original version, each taking a life of its own in a process of free association.

One cannot predict where this will lead, because one cannot know what kind of mental connections people may have when they hear an idea. For example, free associations were key to creating the famous Otpor slogan: "He's Finished." It was used in the campaign leading up to presidential elections in 2000, in which incumbent president of Serbia Slobodan Milosevic was defeated, which ultimately led to his downfall a few weeks later. The slogan for this campaign was developed at one of the brainstorming sessions where one of the activists saw the acronym GOTV for "Get out to Vote" which resembles GOToV je — he's finished in Serbian. And thus the slogan was born. It is still one of the most remembered slogans in the history of Serbian political campaigns.

After a sufficient number of ideas has been generated, the group can proceed to further developing ideas, giving them form and describing them in greater detail. This can be done individually or in small groups, and people can pick their own or someone else's ideas and develop them further. Only after this stage can you finally pass judgment—offer comments, criticism, and suggestions for improvement.

This refinement phase is where ideas are developed into workable solutions for different elements of your campaign. Each carries the campaign message and results in behavioral changes, however small, of different segments on the Spectrum of Allies. These refined ideas can then be selected using a Cost/Benefit Analysis, with the purpose of determining the costs in terms of human and material resources, the time it would take to organize and implement them, and risks associated with each idea. The benefits are determined by looking at the campaign message and desired behavioral changes of the target audience.

Brainstorming cannot and should not be used to select tactics or make more general decisions regarding campaign messaging. Campaign messaging is the result of an analytical process and is developed using the Spectrum of Allies and Perception Box tools, while tactics generated during Brainstorming must be selected using the Cost/Benefit Analysis. Brainstorming thus serves as a creative interlude between stakeholder analysis and selection which checks these tactics against the previously conducted stakeholder analysis.

Brainstorming creates the best results if conducted regularly, even if most ideas generated by this exercise turn out not to be very useful. But as time progresses, new opportunities arise and some of the ideas become more useful and applicable under new circumstances.

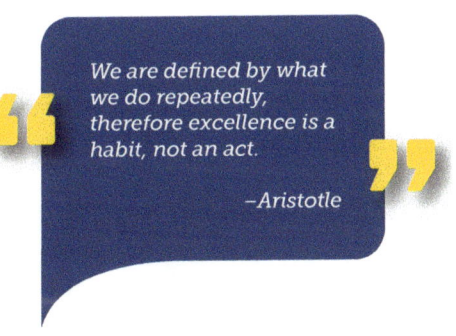

We are defined by what we do repeatedly, therefore excellence is a habit, not an act.

–Aristotle

Instruction Sheet

Brainstorming			
Analytical	Small Group Work	No Handout	75 minutes

Quick Summary

Task	Activity	Time (min)
1. Introduce the tool	Presentation	5
2. Generate ideas	Brainstorming	20
3. Develop ideas	Individual work or work in pairs/small groups	15
4. Refine ideas	Group discussion	30
5. Finish the exercise	Wrap-up	5
Total:		**75**

Materials Needed	When	What For
Notebooks	Individual work	Developing ideas
Pens		

Before the Workshop	Before the Session
	Provide access to campaign message, ideally by posting it on the wall of the room

Step-by-Step Process

| 1. Introduce the tool | Presentation | 5 minutes |

Start by telling participants that it is time to be creative. Remind them that, after defining your target audiences and analyzing their perceptions, you can now play with different ideas for tactics, slogans and campaign materials which will communicate your campaign message to these audiences.

Explain the brainstorming process. Let participants know that they will first spend half an hour generating ideas with the aim of creating a large quantity, withholding judgment, and refraining from comments and criticism. The latter will take place later in the process, after enough ideas have been created to be able to select the best from the pool.

Ask if there are any questions. Repeat that the goal of the brainstorming is to generate ideas, aiming for quantity.

| 2. Generate ideas | Brainstorming | 20 minutes |

Invite people to shout out ideas for slogans, tactics, campaign materials, and so on. Follow the discussion, intervening if someone comments on previous ideas and encouraging him/her to build on previous ideas instead. Remind the group that the goal is to generate as many ideas as possible in half an hour.

Half way through the process (after 15 minutes), invite people who haven't spoken yet to share their ideas with the group.

| 3. Develop ideas | Individual/small group work | 15 minutes |

Ask participants to take out their notebook and work individually on their ideas, trying to further develop them. Participants who have very similar ideas can work in pairs or in small groups.

Fifteen minutes into the small group work call them back and ask them to bring their sheets of paper.

| 4. Refine ideas | Group discussion | 30 minutes |

Ask for a volunteer to come forth and quickly present his/her idea. After s/he finishes, ask participants if they have any quick comments or questions, in particular if they want to add something that could improve the idea. If necessary, ask participants to clarify how their idea would be materialized in the context of a campaign—are they presenting a poster, a slogan, a tactic, or something else?

Make sure to postpone any discussion regarding costs and benefits of the presented tactics for later by asking participants to offer only quick comments. Reiterate that the objective of brainstorming is to generate ideas, while the discussion on viability and usefulness of these ideas will take place later.

5. Finish the exercise	Wrap-up	5 minutes

Thank the participants for their input and explain once again the purpose of brainstorming. Give an example from your experience of how brainstorming helped you in your work. Emphasize that creativity unleashed in this session is built on the analytical work conducted in previous sessions and that creativity without analysis can sometimes be wasted. Ask if there are any final questions.

Endnotes

1. Sometimes it is useful to designate one participant with the task of taking notes during initial brainstorming, when ideas are developed, since some of the ideas may be lost if not recorded in that particular moment.

8. COST/BENEFIT ANALYSIS: PICKING THE BEST IDEA

Introduction

Campaign messaging is conveyed through tactics and campaign material. Each tactic and poster or flyer can be used to carry the campaign message, but not all of the brainstormed tactics, posters, and so on do that job equally well. Not all require the same amount of resources. You know that the resources are limited and must be used carefully to maximize the impact of the campaign. For that reason, you must select and prioritize tactics that will be used in the campaign. As a result, you will have a pool of tactics you can then further develop once you engage in tactical planning. You will know why you decided to pick a particular tactic from the pool over its alternatives—because you compared their costs and benefits.

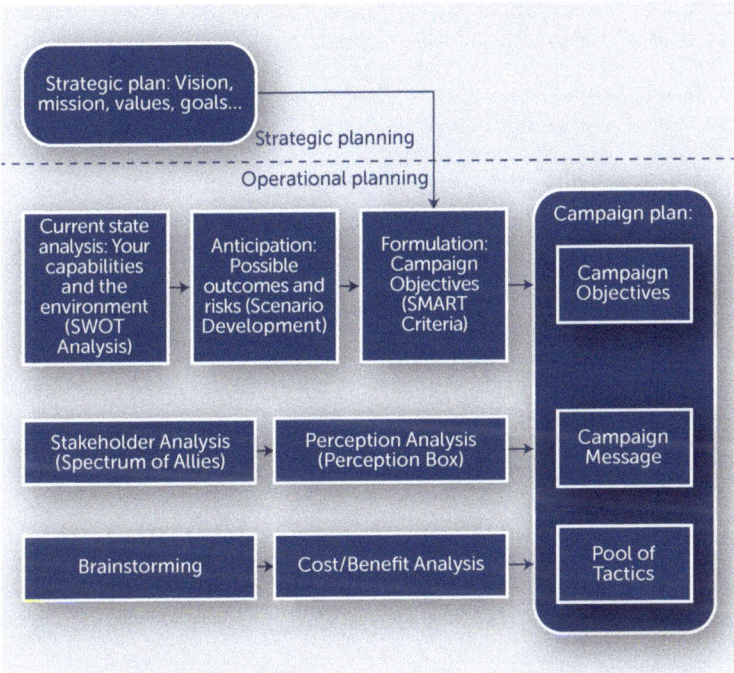

This is why brainstorming should be followed by a Cost/Benefit Analysis. During brainstorming you aimed at quantity, generated a number of ideas, and were not concerned with the resources required. You haven't yet accounted for risks associated with the ideas or the most effective tactics to reach your goal. You did make sure that these ideas for tactics, slogans, and so on conveyed the campaign message, but you didn't assess how well they will do that, especially from a comparative standpoint. But in the course of campaign implementation, you will have to choose tactics that will have greater impact for the same cost, since most campaigns are working with limited resources.

Cost/Benefit Analysis can be extensive and examples from the business world show you how thorough it can be. Campaigns in the context of movements are different than those in the context of business. Movement-related campaigns can rally outside supporters and volunteers to utilize their resources, thus amplifying the campaign message. When you launch a campaign, you hope that people supporting it will spread its message further without officially joining the campaign team. A campaign could then go viral without being limited by the capabilities of the organization that launched it. Still, you need to have an idea of the costs and benefits of the tactics, execute lower cost tactics first, and leave higher cost tactics for later, when the campaign catches on and your capabilities increase.

Simple Cost/Benefit Analysis in your case is a group estimate of costs and benefits of tactics that came out of brainstorming. It relies on the wisdom of crowds and grassroots, on collective opinions of a group of individuals rather than that of a single expert. It has been observed that this collective estimation cancels out deviations of each individual and produces estimates that are as good as, and sometimes better than, estimates made by qualified individual experts. An interesting account of this phenomenon was given in a book by James Surowiecki, titled *The Wisdom of Crowds*.

In order to get an idea of costs and benefits associated with tactics developed in a brainstorming session, each tactic is presented separately to the group conducting Cost/Benefit Analysis. Each participant in the analysis independently estimates the cost of the presented tactic and its benefit. The cost estimate covers such items as:

- Necessary resources (human resources, material resources and time needed to plan and execute the tactic);

- Necessary organizational capacity (skills required, coordination needed to execute the tactic);

- Risks associated with the tactic such as violence (probability of repression, target audience's violent response or violence caused by radical flanks within the campaign);

- Costs to reputation, cohesion, enthusiasm, etc., of the campaign team.

In the benefits estimation you primarily look at how well a tactic carries the campaign message and to what extent it influences the behavior of the target group in the desired direction (according to the Spectrum of Allies). Some other factors to take into consideration are:

- Does it have any ripple effects on other groups, besides the one that is directly being targeted?

- Does the tactic provide opportunities to recruit new activists?

- Does it strengthen the organization and, if so, to what extent?

- Does it provide opportunities to reach out to other organizations and potentially build coalitions with them?

- Generally, does the tactic under consideration advance the overall strategy of the movement?

Not everyone will be aware of all the costs and all the potential benefits of a tactic. This is why collective wisdom is required. Another factor to keep in mind is that costs can be further reduced and benefits increased once you get into tactical planning. At that point, you can flush out all the details, optimally utilize the resources, reduce the risks, and increase the benefits of a tactic. But at this stage, when you are first coming up with a pool of tactics associated with the campaign you are planning, you need to have a rough idea about costs and benefits to know whether to include the tactic as an option to be executed as part of the campaign.

The purpose of the Cost/Benefit Analysis is to make a distinction between different tactics and to place each of them in one of the following groups:

- low cost/high benefit tactics

- low cost/low benefit tactics

- high cost/high benefit tactics

- high cost/low benefit tactics

Low cost/high benefit tactics are clearly ideal; they offer a great number of benefits in exchange for little cost. They are followed by low cost/low benefit tactics, which are at least cheap in terms of cost, although they might not be the most beneficial. These are followed by high cost/high benefit tactics. This is where you need to draw the line. Some of these tactics will be above the line and you will include them in the pool of possible tactics for your campaign because the benefit is so high it justifies the cost. However, some will not make the cut and you will get rid of them since the cost does not justify the benefit. High cost/low benefit tactics are usually not considered at all.

In order to conduct this analysis, you need to first come up with a scale for both costs and benefits. This can be a simple binary option (high versus low cost, little or no benefit versus substantial benefit) or a more complex scale (1 to 10, for example). The advantage of binary options is that it pushes estimation to extremes, which makes it easier to choose, since you are choosing between two diametrically opposed options. But this method lacks nuance and subtlety, which is why sometimes a more complex scale is more appropriate. At the same time, the problem with more complex scales is that it can place results around the middle, so you may end up having a lot of tactics with costs estimated between 4 and 6, and not a single one estimated at extremes such as 1 or 2 or 9 or 10.

Whichever scale you choose, you need to understand that at the end of the analysis, they need to fall into the four groups mentioned above, even if this means that a tactic estimated at 4.9 falls into low cost, while another one, estimated at 5.1 falls into the high cost segment.

It is useful to have a graph with two axes—one for cost and the other for benefit. You then place every tactic on a graph after a vote on that tactic. The line that divides tactics worth pursuing from those that didn't make it into the pool is arbitrary and can be drawn later, after all the tactics are positioned on the graph. You draw a line in such a way that it leaves out all the tactics whose costs are above a certain value, or whose benefits are below certain value, or any combination of the two. Or you can draw the line in such a way as to leave a number of tactics with certain scores below the line. The ranking does not need to be perfect, but it needs to be made so decisions can follow.

Once you draw the line, you have your pool of tactics to use later in your tactical planning exercise. It is important to keep the tactics that didn't make it into the pool, since they could be potentially reworked later to reduce their cost. They could also serve as an inspiration for low-cost alternatives. Furthermore, perhaps some of the tactics didn't make it into the pool because of their high cost, regardless of the fact that they would benefit the campaign greatly. These tactics, difficult to implement at the start of the campaign, could be easier to execute if the campaign produces momentum and new, unforeseeable options open up.

Instruction Sheet

Cost/Benefit Analysis			
Analytical	Group Work	No Handout	30 minutes

Quick Summary		
Content	**Activity**	**Time** (min)
1. Introduce the tool	Presentation	10
2. Evaluate tactics	Group evaluation	15
3. Finish the exercise	Wrap-up	5
Total:		**30**

Materials Needed	When	What For
Small blackboards, one for each participant	Group evaluation	Evaluating tactics
Chalk		

Before the Workshop	Before the Session
	Provide access to tactics generated during brainstorming. Ideally each participant should have one tactic in his or her notebook.

Step-by-Step Process

| 1. Introduce the tool | Presentation | 10 minutes |

Start by explaining why you are conducting a Cost/Benefit Analysis. Remind the participants that you came up with a number of tactics and refined them. Now you need to evaluate them. Ask if there are any questions.

| 2. Evaluate tactics | Group evaluation | 15 minutes |

Invite people to present their tactics, campaign materials, etc. in a sentence or two. Then ask participants to write a number on the blackboard for the presented tactic: first the cost of the tactic and then the benefit. After a few seconds, ask them to calculate the average values for both cost and benefit. Position the tactic on the Cost/Benefit graph so that the x value corresponds to cost and y value to benefit. Repeat the process for each tactic.

After 15 minutes or, ideally, after all the tactics have been evaluated, thank everybody for their input and show them the Cost/Benefit graph with all the tactics positioned on it.

| 3. Finish the exercise | Wrap-up | 5 minutes |

Draw a line on the Cost/Benefit Graph which divides tactics into two categories: those with higher cost and lower benefit and those with lower cost and higher benefit. The line could be diagonal and at an equal distance from both axes, forming a 45-degree angle with them (as shown on the next page), or its angle could be completely arbitrary and drawn to divide all the tactics into two relatively equal groups.

Read the list of tactics that made it above the dividing line. Ask a volunteer to take notes.

Thank everyone and explain that all the elements needed for a campaign plan are now in place. Congratulate them on their work. End the session.

Endnotes

1. Cost/Benefit Graph (see image below).

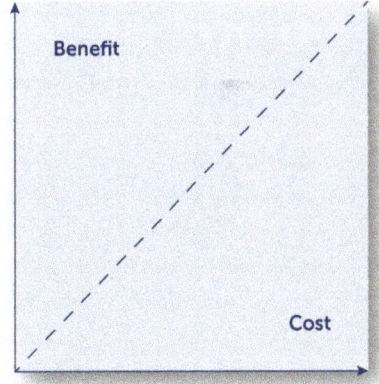

9. CAMPAIGN PLAN: PUTTING IT ALL ON PAPER

Introduction

The campaign plan is an internal document that you as a campaign team use for reference, but that you also use to recruit people to your campaign, to ask for assistance and resources, to negotiate with other stakeholders, and to build coalitions around your campaign. It is a relatively short document that can be condensed into four sections:

1. Campaign Objectives
2. Campaign Message
3. Tactics
4. Organization and Resources

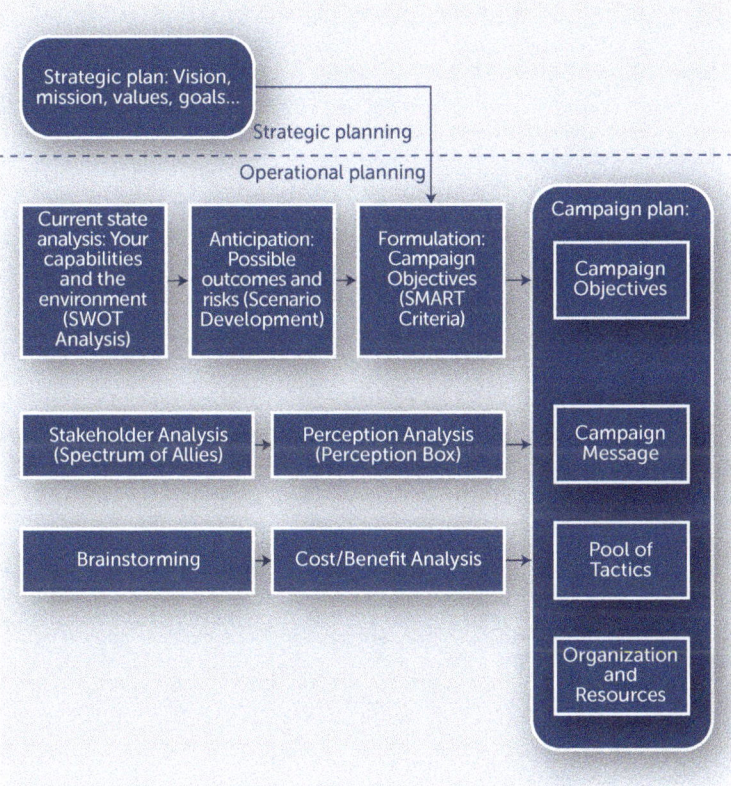

The first section, campaign objectives, ensures that they satisfy SMART criteria. They need to be specific, measurable, achievable, relevant, and time-bound. This section of the campaign plan tells you what you want to achieve with your campaign, as well as why you want to achieve it. You also look at how your objective is relevant to the wider strategy, and how it gets you closer to your long-term goals, defined in the strategic plan.

The second section focuses on the message. It tells you who you target with your message, what kind of behavioral change you want to see, and what specifically and how you are going to communicate to these target audiences. This section is informed by the stakeholder analysis conducted earlier and uses the developed campaign message in the form of talking points.

The third section lists tactics that will be executed in the course of the campaign, material to be used, and any other methods that might be used to convey the campaign message. This section also provides information about the timeline of the campaign, phases, and buildup. It also defines how and when the campaign will end.

The fourth and final section addresses organizational capacity and resources that will be needed to implement the campaign. It estimates the quantity of campaign material, number of volunteers and organizers needed to run the campaign and execute tactics, time needed to set up and implement the campaign, as well as other resources, including funds needed to support the campaign organization. This section also specifies decision making, the extent of local autonomy, and internal communication.

Once completed, the campaign plan can later be used to develop other documents needed to fully define the campaign you developed. These documents include:

- Campaign brief
- Campaign calendar
- Campaign budget
- Campaign organizational scheme

A campaign brief is a more detailed document than the campaign plan. It is a technical document, usually prepared by clients for marketing agencies as a type of instruction. It tells the agency what you want to achieve with your campaign, who you will target, and what your message will be. It lays out deadlines and milestones and provides them with a projected budget. Agencies respond to this with a so-called creative brief, which is their take on all the elements in the campaign brief (objective, target, message, etc.) together with a proposed schedule and additional requests they may have from the client.

Campaign Plan
(Template)

Background:

Who is launching the campaign and what is the campaign issue? How is the issue connected to your vision and mission?

Objective:

What specific objectives do you want to achieve with your campaign? How are you going to measure the success of the campaign? Why do you believe these objectives are achievable? How is it relevant to your wider strategy? How long will the campaign last?

Message:

Who are you targeting with your campaign? What groups and social demographics do you aim to influence? What kind of behavioral change of the target audiences do you want to see as a result of your campaign?

What will you say? What message will you convey? What is your tone? How is this supported by your strategic communication (your vision, mission, and values)?

What is the main slogan of the campaign? What are some other slogans or visuals that could be used?

Tactics:

What tactics (or what kinds of tactics) are you going to have in the campaign? What campaign material will be produced? What will the campaign launch look like? What phases will follow the launch? What tactics and campaign material will be used in each phase? How will the campaign end? Are there any potential tactics to be used if opportunities arise?

Resources:

How many volunteers, activists, and organizers will be needed for the successful implementation of the campaign? What material resources will be needed for campaign implementation? What is the timeline of the campaign? When does it start and when does it end? What logistical support is needed to support the campaign?

Organization:

What are the roles, duties, and responsibilities, and how are they distributed? How are decisions made? What are the channels for internal communication? What level of autonomy does an activist have inside the campaign? In what ways can people support the campaign?

Organizations may decide not to ask external marketing agencies for help, but they could still develop a campaign brief for their creative teams to use as a reference when developing campaign material and for tactical planning. A campaign brief can be devised from the campaign plan. The main difference between the two is the level of detail, since the campaign brief is prepared for people who have little or no knowledge of the organization behind the campaign and the planning process by which the campaign plan was developed.

Another document that should be prepared following the campaign plan is the detailed campaign calendar. It shows the campaign start and end dates, as well as phases of the campaign between the launch and conclusion. Tactics are spread out during this period in such a way as to build momentum of the campaign, and deadlines for completing campaign material and distribution are as well.

The campaign budget specifies projected costs of the campaign, including everything from the cost of executing tactics, producing and distributing campaign material, and media buying down to logistical costs in support of the campaign organization (communication, transportation, meals, payments, and so on).

The campaign organization scheme is a type of work flow document and visually shows who is making what decisions in the campaign, how communication channels look, and who is responsible for what in the campaign, such as work with volunteers, public relations, finances, and legal issues.

Apart from these documents, the campaign plan can be used to develop a short pitch sometimes called the "elevator pitch." This is used to persuade sympathetic individuals and groups (passive allies segment on the Spectrum of Allies) to support the campaign. The reason why it's called an elevator pitch is that it is very concise and can be delivered during a short elevator ride. Imagine you are entering an elevator and an important potential ally is standing next to you. You have less than a minute to hook that person's interest in supporting the campaign.

All the information for the elevator pitch is derived from the campaign plan. It condenses the plan into a few sentences with an inviting and intriguing tone. It is informed by an understanding of your audience's perceptions (see the Perception Box for passive allies).

If the elevator pitch creates interest and the person wants to learn more, all the answers to potential questions can be derived from the campaign plan, most importantly how the person can help and support the campaign.

The elevator pitch should be practiced and, once perfected, could be used in a number of occasions, from official gatherings and informal parties to possibly even actual elevator rides.

Instruction Sheet

Campaign Plan			
Analytical	Group Work	Handout	30 minutes

Quick Summary

Task	Activity	Time (min)
1. Introduce the tool	Presentation	5
2. Divide participants in four small groups	Division exercise	5
3. Write segments of the campaign plan	Small group work	30
4. Present the campaign plan	Presentation and discussion	15
5. Finish the exercise	Wrap-up	5
Total:		**60**

Materials Needed	When	What For
Pens	Small group work	Writing campaign plan
Campaign Plan Handout		

Before the Workshop	Before the Session
	Provide access to the campaign objective, campaign message and a pool of tactics (ideally these are posted on the wall of the room).

Step-by-Step Process

1. Introduce the tool	Presentation	5 minutes

Start by explaining the purpose of the campaign plan. Remind the participants that you have the objective of the campaign, the campaign message, and a pool of tactics and that these need to be put into one document: the campaign plan. This plan will be used as a reference point as you develop your campaign further, create materials for the campaign, implement tactics, or organize events.

Distribute the campaign plan handout. Explain each section of the plan, starting from the segment that states the campaign objectives. Then move on to the part of the plan that deals with message, followed by the segment that lists potential tactics, and finally the remaining two sections that cover resources needed for the campaign and campaign organization. Tell participants that they need to fill in each section of the campaign plan by answering the questions listed in the handout and taking into account all the work that was previously done on objectives, messaging, and tactics.

2. Divide participants in small groups	Division exercise	5 minutes

Ask participants to line up based on the time they usually wake up in the morning. Have those who wake up early toward one end of the line and those who like to sleep later toward the other. After they have finished lining up, divide participants into four small groups with late risers covering the campaign objective, the next group covering campaign message, the next covering tactics, and finally, the last group of participants who wake up early covering campaign resources and organization.

3. Write segments of the campaign plan	Small group work	30 minutes

Inform each group which segment of the campaign plan they should develop. Explain that they should feel free to send an emissary to another group if they need to consult with them. Let them know that they have 30 minutes for this and that after they write their section of the plan, they will do a presentation and engage in a discussion. Stress that this will not be the final version of the campaign plan, since these segments would need to be compiled into one document that will probably need some additional work thereafter.

As groups begin work, walk around and ask if there are any questions, providing guidance if necessary. Make another round 10 minutes later and a final round 10 minutes before the end, asking each group to wrap up and get ready for presentation. After 30 minutes ask participants to finish their work and present the plan.

4. Present the campaign plan	Presentation and discussion	15 minutes

Ask a representative from each group to present their segment of the campaign plan, starting with objectives, followed by message, tactics, resources, and organization. After all the groups have presented, open the floor for discussion. Conclude after 15 minutes.

5. Finish the exercise	Wrap-up	5 minutes

Thank the participants for their input and explain once again the purpose of the campaign plan. Explain that the document will need some additional work in order to be complete. Ask if there are any final questions.

10. TACTICS

Introduction

What is a tactic? The root of the word is the Greek "taktikē" which means the "(art of) arrangement" of military forces. Like "campaigns," this word comes from military vocabulary and is used as a concept in business and politics. Soldiers talk about tactics such as ambush, skirmish, or siege. Salespeople talk about discounting, rebates, and "Buy one, get one free" offers. And members of parliament talk about motions, amendments, and the filibuster.

Tactics of civil resistance—such as strikes, boycotts, civil disobedience, and many other actions—are the most exciting part of civil resistance, even when they are isolated events. But when tactics are sequenced as part of a campaign, they produce maximum impact. They build on each other, increase participation, build momentum, and influence a variety of audiences. They are powerful.

Devising effective tactics, and designing tactical sequences, can be a challenge. People need to be stimulated to think outside the box, since, by default, they tend to repeat tactics they are most comfortable with and may hesitate to experiment with new ones.

However, once you have chosen your tactics, planning them is a relatively straightforward matter. If you have a developed campaign plan, you already know the objective of the campaign, you have the campaign message, and you have already identified potential allies, capacities, and resources that might be involved in certain tactics. Once we understand how our tactic fits the wider campaign, we need to see how we can be innovative with our tactical selection.

Tactical Innovation

As mentioned, a core challenge in tactical planning is innovation—coming up with novel tactics. Once tactics are conceived, they are developed in a simple and straightforward process; but devising a tactic requires creativity, effort, and inspiration. Researching the target of the tactic, positioning this target on the Spectrum of Allies and understanding the reasons of that position using Perception Box are very important. This will help you to not only understand the target better but it will give you ideas for tactics. When you do your research, you will discover more options and potential points of intervention. Once you have done this, there are three practices which will help you come up with imaginative ideas for tactics. These practices are:

- Collection
- Brainstorming

- Experimentation

Collection is the practice of gathering information about tactics used in the past, in other countries, or in the same country by some other group. Inspiration could be gotten from newspaper articles, books, and movies. Recently it has become easier than ever to find examples of tactics thanks to online sharing through blogposts, videos, and even livestreams. But here lies the danger: inspiration can sometimes lead to mere copying, and a tactic, transplanted from one place to another without adjustments to fit the new context, can fail or backfire. Every tactic, therefore, needs to be adjusted to the local context. In order to make that adjustment, we need to understand the original context where the tactic was used. As one aspect of this, for example, tactics have different symbolic meanings in different countries, so instead of copying the tactic from another country we should, through research, understand the symbolic importance of the tactic in the specific history of that country. Once we understand that, we can try to find a different tactic with a similar symbolic meaning in our context.

Brainstorming, as we explain earlier in the book, produces best results when it is conducted regularly. Here we emphasize that quantity leads to quality—many ideas generated at brainstorming sessions could be useless, but they lead to other new ideas that may be more effective in carrying the campaign forward. Collection of past tactics also helps make brainstorming produce more creative tactics as some of these ideas improve as they get refined over time. Through informed brainstorming, ideas become viable. Sometimes the context changes and some of the ideas that initially seemed weak suddenly become viable.

Experimentation is another practice that can make tactics more effective in the long run. As all tactics have a local context, we can try certain tactics in small towns and, if they work, we can use them again in big cities where press coverage will amplify their effect. If a certain tactic flops, it is still possible to learn from the failed experiment to understand why it didn't make the desired impact.

Tactical Sequencing

We intuitively know that repeating the same tactic repeatedly is not very effective. In fact, when we examine tactical implementation over time, we discover it is much like breathing. Inhaling is followed by exhaling, tactics of concentration (which gather people closely in one place) are best followed by tactics of dispersion (which take place over a wide area), high-risk tactics by low-risk tactics. Large gatherings in one location like marches and rallies may be followed by tactics where people do not congregate in the same spot but gather in their neighborhoods or sometimes engage from their homes. If you ask people to attend rallies every day, inevitably there will be days with lower turnout and people might start wondering if the movement is declining. If after a successful rally people are asked to gather in their neighborhoods, they will carry the energy and enthusiasm there and even recruit some of their neighbors. Tactics of dispersion also keep the opponent in check as it is harder to send a special police unit to try to suppress widespread localized resistance than it is to crush demonstrations taking place at the central square.

This is why, when we engage in tactical planning, we have to take into consideration previous tactics we have used and ask ourselves how a planned tactic will fit into the sequence, how will it contribute to that sequence, and how will it build momentum and advance the campaign's message and goals.

Tactical Planning

Tactics carry the campaign message, so we need to find the best tactic for the job. We start by picking a tactic from the pool of tactics that we brainstormed and ranked based on their estimated cost and benefit (described in the chapters on brainstorming and Cost/Benefit Analysis). In making this choice we also consider the importance of innovation and sequencing. We then need to plan the tactic at a level of detail that is much greater than anything we planned at the campaign level.

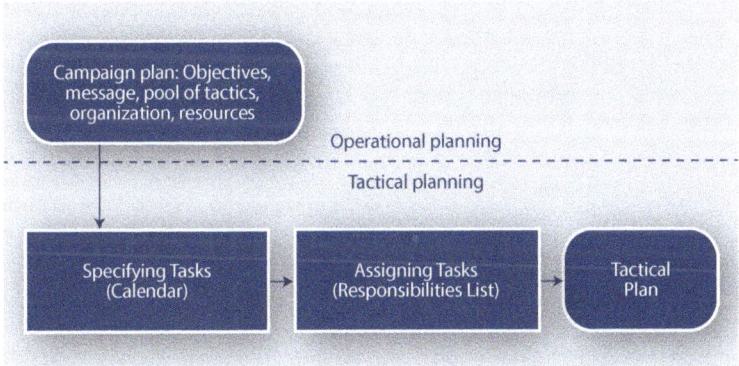

First we need to turn our tactic from an idea into a series of manageable tasks which—when executed in the right order—produce the intended effect.

Then we need to put these tasks on a calendar, determine when the tactic starts and when it ends, knowing that from a planner's perspective a tactic starts earlier and ends later than from the perspective of an observer. For instance, a rally that you plan may be a one-day event for those attending, but for planners and organizers "the rally tactic" starts weeks before "the rally event." "The rally tactic" may also end days or weeks after "the rally event" when we still may be publishing articles about the event and training people we recruited at the event. Together, all of these tasks constitute "the rally tactic" and create an impact, although to the outside observer only "the rally event" may be visible.

When we turn a tactic into a series of tasks, we need to think about every aspect of organizing it, from essential tasks to marginal details. Bringing loudspeakers to a rally is essential, while dropping a banner from a nearby building is marginal, although that may be nice to have. To concentrate our energy and resources, we need to distinguish between absolutely necessary tasks (without which the tactic will fail) from other tasks that will make the tactic more effective, more memorable, or more fun. We should mark essential tasks as we create our "to do" list as it will help us later when we put the tasks on the calendar and assign them to people who will be in charge of carrying them out.

When we put tasks on a calendar, we use a process called "reverse planning." We start this process by identifying the date of the central event which outside observers will be able to notice. If the tactic is centered around an event or an important symbolic date, we start with that. If there is no such requirement, then we can determine the date based on availability of resources and organizational capacity—we will plan the tactic when we have available time, human and material resources. Once we have identified the date of the central event, we determine the immediate essential tasks that must be implemented ahead of time in order for the event to happen. Tasks that must happen in the week directly before the event are placed on the calendar first and cover what is called "event week." Then, going back further, we populate the week before event week with the necessary preceding tasks. Then we list tasks that need to happen even earlier. The tactic begins with these earliest tasks, at least from the planner's perspective, although these may look insignificant to an outside observer.

After we are done with reverse planning and have posted on the calendar all the tasks that are to take place before the event, we identify the tasks which will happen after the event. This includes all the activities that will need to be implemented immediately after the event to those that may happen a week or more later that amplify the impact of the event. When these tasks are complete we can say that the tactic has ended, at least from the perspective of planners and organizers.

Tactic Calendar								
Even earlier	List tasks which need to be completed as part of early preparation: 1. _____ 2. _____ 3. _____ ...							
	M	T	W	T	F	S	S
1 week before event week								
Event week					Reverse Planning	Event		
1 week after event week								
Even later	List tasks which can be completed later than one week: 1. _____ 2. _____ 3. _____ ...							

When we put tasks on the calendar we should observe how the tasks are spread out. Some of the tasks here will run simultaneously while others will follow sequentially, but they should all be spread out evenly so that we do not have days when we are idle followed by days when our organization is overstretched. It is a good idea to have tasks written on sticky notes that we can move around on the calendar to make sure that we do not have some days with too many sticky notes and others with none.

Once the tasks are listed on the calendar, we assign them to people who will be responsible for their completion. Here we can also note anything of importance related to the task that the assigned person should know. For example, does the task require special resources or skills, or does it entail a particular kind of risk?

Responsibilities List		
Task	Assigned to	Important Information
1. _____		
2. _____		
3. _____		
...		

The calendar together with the listed responsibilities constitute the tactical plan. It contains the essential shared information that we need as a team when planning and implementing a tactic. People responsible for specific tasks may create their own additional plans to help them with implementation, but the tactical plan is something the whole team needs to have access to. Someone should be in charge of overseeing the overall implementation of the tactical plan. This person monitors the status of various tasks and regularly shares progress updates with the whole group, raising an alarm whenever there is a problem. It also helps to have regular short meetings with the whole team that is implementing the tactical plan.

Finally, after the tactical plan has been finalized but before implementation starts, we will want to organize a simulation of the planned tactic where members of the team can practice carrying out the tasks, playing different roles, and getting a sense of what they might encounter when they implement the tactic. Sometimes this simulation can help us identify and plan for various contingencies, which is discussed in the next section.

Simulation

We understand that tactics need to be planned in order to be effective, but there are many factors that increase their effectiveness that cannot be planned—for example, a passionate speech, a catchy chant, a powerful moment caught on video that spreads online, and other factors that are intangible and elusive and not fully under our control. The fact that implementation with all its aspects cannot be fully controlled does not mean that it cannot be practiced and improved upon.

This is where simulation comes in handy. Simulation is an imitation of a situation or process that can be used to teach someone how to do something. In our case, the simulation of a tactic is a sort of dress rehearsal, a dry run in which implementation of the tactic is practiced and possible outcomes are experienced, processed, and internalized by the participants. It does not fully capture the tactic which is being simulated but it gives participants a feel for how the tactic may play out.

For a successful simulation it is important to set the stage and divide up roles using the tactical plan. Now people who are responsible for various tasks can practice implementing them. It is also important to assign roles as those people we may interact with or encounter when we carry out the tactic, such as our opponent, our opponent's supporters, journalists, and bystanders. This creates a more dynamic simulation.

A simulation does not need to take long to play out and can be intense and lively, with a lot of laughs and memorable moments. All these are important as they allow participants to experience a variety of situations they may encounter, process them emotionally and intellectually, and internalize them so that they are prepared if they encounter a similar situation later on.

For a simulation to be successful, it is also important to spare some time for discussion after the simulation is over. This is where everyone involved in the simulation gets to share their experiences, compare them and draw conclusions. It helps participants to internalize these experiences and prepares them for situations they will find themselves in when they implement the tactic.

Apart from tactical preparation, simulations can also be used to prepare people for media interviews, arrests and interrogations, public speeches in hostile environments, negotiations, and all kinds of situations where preparedness is key to an effective response.

Instruction Sheet

Tactical Planning			
Creative	Small Group Work	Handout	90 minutes

Quick Summary

Task	Activity	Time (min)
1. Introduce the tactic	Presentation	10
2. List tasks	Small group work	30
3. Post tasks on the tactic calendar	Group work	20
4. Assign tasks	Group work	15
5. Write down the tactical plan	Individual work	10
6. Conclude the exercise	Wrap-up	5
Total:		**90**

Materials Needed | When | What For

Materials Needed	When	What For
Pre-made sheet with tactic calendar	Small group work	Posting tasks
Sticky notes		
Bowl (or open box)		
Pre-made sheet with responsibilities list	Group work	Assigning tasks
Tactical Plan Handout	Individual work	Writing down tactical plan
Pens		

Before the Workshop | Before the Session

Before the Workshop	Before the Session
Select tactic from the pool of tactics in the campaign plan before the tactic planning workshop starts.	Provide access to the campaign plan.

Step-by-Step Process

1. Introduce the tactic	Presentation	10 minutes

Welcome participants to the tactical planning session. Introduce the tactic selected from the pool of tactics in the campaign plan. Explain how this tactic fits into the larger campaign and how it will carry the campaign message. Ask if there are any questions or comments.

Explain that we are starting with a tactic developed in our brainstorming session and scrutinized using a Cost/Benefit Analysis. Now we need to turn it into a series of manageable tasks. As these tasks are implemented in the right order, the tactic will be carried out.

2. List tasks	Small group work	30 minutes

Divide participants into small groups. Each group should have an even number of participants. Ask groups to sit at separate tables or to scatter around. After they have done this, ask each participant to take out a pen and paper and spend 5 minutes listing tasks which are necessary or helpful for the tactic to be successfully carried out.

After 5 minutes, ask participants to turn to the person next to them and discuss in pairs the tasks they listed and try to come up with one list of tasks. Give them 5 minutes for this.

After 5 minutes, ask the participants to discuss the tasks in their small groups and come up with one task list for each small group. Give them 10 minutes for this. Walk around to check if there are any questions or need for clarification. After the 10 minutes invite them back.

Call each group to read the list of tasks they came up with. After they have done this, ask if there are tasks that are similar or identical and if they can be merged. Allow for a few comments and then ask for two volunteers: one to write the list of tasks on a pre-made sheet with the responsibilities list and the other to write them on the sticky notes and put them in a bowl.

3. Post tasks on the tactic calendar	Group work	20 minutes

Ask participants to take sticky notes from the bowl and post them on the calendar. Encourage them to mingle, talk to each other, move sticky notes around, argue why the task should be implemented on a particular date but also be ready to be convinced otherwise.

Give them up to 20 minutes for this, but closely follow the group dynamics as they work on the calendar and intervene if there is no progress. End the exercise early if you notice consensus in the group and then move to the next step. If they have not finished after 20 minutes, ask the group to leave the tasks as they are on the calendar and proceed to the next step.

4. Assign tasks	Group work	15 minutes

Now that the tasks are on the calendar, tell the participants that they will be assigned to people who will be responsible for implementing them. Ask for volunteers willing to be responsible for a task. Every time a participant volunteers to be responsible for a task, write their name next to the task on the responsibilities list. Continue this until there are no more volunteers or no more tasks which are unassigned. If, after 15 minutes, there are still unassigned tasks, propose to the group that they should have an additional meeting dedicated to completing the responsibilities list. This additional meeting could be completed during a break or in an extra session at the end of the day.

5. Write down the tactical plan	Individual work	10 minutes

Distribute the tactical plan handout. Explain the sections of the plan, starting with the calendar and moving to the responsibilities list that designates people responsible for the execution of each task. Give them 10 minutes to fill the plan.

6. Conclude the exercise	Wrap-up	5 minutes

Thank the participants for their work, tell them that this is the tactical plan they will refer to when they implement the tactic and that will help them track the tasks related to the tactic and who's responsible for carrying them out.

Endnotes

1. An example of reverse planning:

Let's say we want to organize a dinner party. We decide on the date: Saturday two weeks from now. First we come up with a list of tasks which need to be carried out if we want the dinner to happen. Some of these tasks are essential (like inviting people), some are important (like buying drinks), while some would be nice (like reminding people to come and later thanking them for coming). But it is important to list them all and mark those which are essential:

- Create menu
- Cook food*
- Buy groceries*
- Buy drinks
- Invite people*
- Create a guest list
- Remind people about the dinner
- Thank people for coming
- Clean the house

Now that we have a list of tasks we can put them on the calendar starting from the day of the dinner and going backwards. Once we finish with the tasks preceding the dinner, we can put tasks on the calendar which should happen after the dinner. At the end we will have something like this:

	Tactic Calendar						
Even earlier	List tasks which need to be completed as part of early preparation: 1. Create a guest list 2. _____ 3. _____ ...						
	M	T	W	T	F	S	S
1 week before event week					Invite people	Create menu	
Event week		Clean the house	Remind people	Buy drinks	Buy groceries	Cook food **Dinner**	Thank people
1 week after event week	Eat leftovers						
Even later	List tasks which can be completed later than one week: 1. _____ 2. _____ 3. _____ ...						

11. CAMPAIGN DEVELOPMENT COURSE

Introduction

Teaching people how to plan campaigns takes time and effort. But it pays off, because once they learn these tools, they can use them with ease to plan their campaigns. The tools presented in this book can be used for a two-day Campaign Development Course aimed at teaching people how to develop a plan for their campaigns.

A Campaign Development Course progresses slowly, step by step. Each step is informed by our learning objectives, the specific skills or knowledge we would like participants to acquire, and constraints in terms of available time for the course, location, number of participants, and so forth.

Quick Overview of the Course for the Trainer(s)

We open the course by stating its overall aim: to teach participants how to use various planning tools to develop a campaign. Then we refine the aim to teaching participants how to use various planning tools to set campaign objectives, craft its message, develop tactics, and finally, write a campaign plan.

Next, we look at each element of our overall aim and figure out what will be required. To develop the campaign objectives, participants will need to analyze the environment and their capabilities, allowing them to understand the current state in terms of external and internal factors. This provides a snapshot of the current state of affairs. The ability to foresee the interplay of external and internal factors will also allow them to identify different options and take risks into account before formulating objectives. This will help them stay on course in any future scenario. To recap, to set campaign objectives properly, participants must:

- List all the relevant factors
- Develop different scenarios
- Come up with concrete objectives

Then we move to developing the campaign message, and participants identify different groups, understand their perceptions, then come up with an appropriate message. To recap, to craft the campaign message properly, participants will need to:

- List all the relevant stakeholders
- Identify their perceptions
- Come up with an adequate message

Furthermore, participants must learn how to develop tactics that convey the campaign message. They must also learn how to select tactics that achieve this in the most efficient manner, discarding any tactics that don't make this cut. Finally, they must learn how to write a campaign plan to put everything they have created into a coherent document.

Before they can achieve this, participants will need to understand campaigns as a concept. This is not a practical skill, but it is an important part of building knowledge about campaigns.

Now that we understand the process better, we can list learning objectives:

- Explain the role and importance of campaigns in the wider strategic context
- Use SWOT Analysis to list internal and external factors
- Develop scenarios to explore options and understand risks
- Set campaign objectives using SMART criteria
- Analyze stakeholders and their perceptions
- Craft campaign message in the form of talking points
- Select tactics based on their costs and benefits
- Write a campaign plan

Planning the Course

In order to reach these eight learning objectives, we will need roughly eight units of 90 minutes each. Equal length of units ensures that the course is well paced but there is still enough time for breaks to help participants be more attentive and productive during sessions.

On the next page you will see what the course curriculum will look like in concrete terms after we match modules to units. Note that this schedule includes additional time at the beginning of the course to break the ice, introduce ourselves (trainers and participants), provide an overview of the course, cover housekeeping tasks (administrative, logistical), and so on. A segment at the end of the course was also added to allow some time for questions, course evaluation, and discussion about next steps. Activities have also been added here and there to make the information flow smoothly and allow participants to actually plan a campaign—not just learn how to use the various planning tools.

Campaign Development Course Curriculum

Unit	Time	Module	Time
Introduction to campaigns	90	Opening activities	30
		Introduction to campaigns	30
		Overview of the strategic plan/campaign issue	30
Overview of external and internal factors	90	Opening activities	15
		Preparation for SWOT Analysis	15
		SWOT Analysis	60
Exploring options, understanding risks	90	Scenario Development	90
Campaign objectives	90	Listing broad campaign aims	30
		SMART Criteria	30
		Setting concrete campaign objectives	30
Stakeholder analysis	90	Spectrum of Allies	30
		Perception Box	60
Campaign message	90	Talking Points	30
		Brainstorming	60
Tactics	90	Introduction to tactics	30
		Developing tactics	30
		Cost/Benefit Analysis	30
Campaign plan	90	Developing campaign plan	60
		Evaluation, feedback, next steps	30

Now we can use this information to build a two-day course overview:

Course title	Campaign Development Course
Aim	The aim of this course is to teach participants how to use various planning tools to plan a campaign.
Learning objectives	At the end of this course, participants will be able to: • Explain the role and importance of campaigns in the wider strategic context • Use SWOT Analysis to list internal and external factors • Develop scenarios to explore options and understand risks • Set campaign objectives using SMART criteria • Analyze stakeholders and their perceptions • Craft campaign message in the form of talking points • Select tactics based on their costs and benefits • Write a campaign plan
Time	Total time: 960 minutes (16 hours) Classroom time: 720 minutes (12 hours) Breaks: 240 minutes (4 hours)
Materials	Pre-made slides: PS-1/CDC (Strategy Pyramid), PS-2/CDC (SWOT Matrix), PS-3/CDC (Scenario Matrix), PS-4/CDC (Gandhi's Letter), PS-5/CDC (Spectrum of Allies), PS-6/CDC (Perception Box) Handouts: HO-1/CDC (Scenario Matrix), HO-2/CDC (SMART Criteria Handout), HO-3/CDC (Campaign Plan Template) Flip chart and permanent markers Whiteboard and erasable markers Adhesive tape Notebooks and pens Sticky notes

The agenda for the course would look like this:

Two-day Campaign Development Course Agenda		
Day one		
09:00-10:30	Introduction to campaigns (presentation, discussion)	90 min
10:30-11:00	Break	30
11:00-12:30	Overview of external and internal factors (SWOT Analysis)	90
12:30-13:30	Lunch	60
13:30-15:00	Exploring options, understanding risks (Scenario Development)	90
15:00-15:30	Break	30
15:30-17:00	Setting campaign objectives (SMART Criteria)	90
Day two		
09:00-10:30	Stakeholder analysis (Spectrum of Allies, Perception Box)	90
10:30-11:00	Break	30
11:00-12:30	Crafting campaign message (Talking Points)	90
12:30-13:30	Lunch	60
13:30-15:00	Building a pool of tactics (Brainstorming, Cost/Benefit Analysis)	90
15:00-15:30	Break	30
15:30-17:00	Developing a campaign plan (group work, presentation, discussion)	90

The course could also be delivered during a weekend workshop. This is usually done for people who have weekday jobs and therefore cannot afford to take a course during the week. In this case, the workshop would start on Friday evening and end on Sunday around lunchtime.

The agenda would look like this:

Weekend Campaign Development Course Agenda		
Day one (Friday)		
20:00-21:30	Introduction to campaigns (presentation, discussion)	90
Day two (Saturday)		
9:00-10:30	Overview of external and internal factors (SWOT Analysis)	90
10:30-11:00	Break	30
11:00-12:30	Exploring options, understanding risks (Scenario Development)	90
12:30-13:30	Lunch	60
13:30-15:00	Setting campaign objectives (SMART Criteria)	90
15:00-15:30	Break	30
15:30-17:00	Stakeholder analysis (Spectrum of Allies, Perception Box)	90
17:00-20:00	Dinner and downtime	180
20:00-21:30	Crafting campaign message (Talking Points)	90
Day three (Sunday)		
9:00-10:30	Building a pool of tactics (Brainstorming, Cost/Benefit Analysis)	90
10:30-11:00	Break	30
11:00-12:30	Developing a campaign plan (group work, presentation, discussion)	90
12:30-13:30	Lunch	60

12. TACTICAL PLANNING WORKSHOP

The tactical planning workshop, consisting of tactical plan development and a simulation of the planned tactic, can be done in one afternoon. The components of this workshop are:

Session	Total Time (min)	Module	Time (min)
Tactical plan	90	Specifying tasks	60
		Assigning tasks	15
		Writing the tactical plan	15
Simulation	90	Preparing the simulation	15
		Running the simulation	45
		Debrief	30

Now we can use this information to build a workshop overview:

Course title	Tactical Planning Workshop
Aim	The aim of this workshop is to teach participants how to use various planning tools to plan a tactic.
Learning objectives	At the end of this course, participants will be able to: • Break down tactical planning into a series of manageable tasks • Use the reverse planning technique to populate Tactic Calendar • Write a tactical plan
Time	Total time: 195 minutes (3 ¼ hours) Classroom time: 180 minutes (3 hours) Breaks: 15 minutes (¼ hours)
Materials	Pre-made slides: PS-1/TPW (Tactic Calendar), PS-2/TPW (Responsibilities List) Handouts: HO-1/TPW (Tactical Plan Template) Flip chart and permanent markers Whiteboard and erasable markers Adhesive tape Notebooks and pens Sticky notes Bowl

The agenda for the workshop would look like this:

Evening Tactical Planning Workshop		
18:00-19:30	Tactical plan: Specifying tasks, assigning tasks, and creating the plan	90
19:30-19:45	Break	15
19:45-21:15	Simulation: Preparing, running, and debriefing	90

AFTERWORD

Tools presented in this book break down the campaign planning process into distinct steps, each covering one element of a final campaign plan: campaign objectives, message, tactics, and so on. This is how the difficult and complex task of campaign development is made simpler—*without* simplifying the campaign plan produced as the result of this process.

Plans are worthless but planning is everything.

–Dwight Eisenhower

The campaign plan is the final product of the planning process, but in a way, the process is more important than the result. Sometimes, unforeseen events drastically change the environment in which the campaign is implemented, new opportunities arise, threats materialize, or hidden weaknesses suddenly surface, rendering the campaign plan obsolete. But the information gathered using various tools as part of the planning process equips us with strategic skills that allow us to read and understand the changing environment, adapt to it, and respond quickly and adequately.

The movement you are part of may have been active for only one year, or five years, or 10 years—or perhaps much longer. The movement may be on an adrenaline high from a recent success against its adversary, whether an authoritarian regime, a corrupt system, or an enduring injustice. Or the movement may be stagnating and in despair after having been violently (or otherwise) repressed. The movement may be composed of hundreds of thousands of men, women, elderly, and children from diverse backgrounds, or there may be only a few dozen activists scrambling to grow participation numbers.

Whatever the case may be, it is never too early or too late, too perfect or too poor of timing, too harsh or too ideal of a context, too great or too small of numbers to begin incorporating campaign planning into your community's nonviolent struggle for rights, freedom, and justice.

www.ingramcontent.com/pod-product-compliance
Lightning Source LLC
Chambersburg PA
CBHW041129110526
44592CB00020B/2741